To Ruth,
_my A!_

BOBBING
ABOUT

Bob Burden

ROBERT BURDEN

©Copyright 2000 Robert A Burden

The right of Robert A Burden to be identified as the author of this work has been asserted in accordance with the Copyright, Designs and Patents Act 1988.

All rights reserved. No reproduction, copy or transmission of this publication may be made without written permission. No paragraph of this publication may be reproduced, copied or transmitted save with the written permission or in accordance with the provisions of the Copyright Act 1956 (as amended). Any person who does any unauthorised act in relation to this publication may be liable to criminal prosecution and civil claims for damage.

First published in 2000 by
Cromwell Publishers
Eagle Court Concord Business Park
Threapwood Road Manchester M22 0RR

E-mail: Editorial@CromwellPublishers.co.uk
Web address: www.CromwellPublishers.co.uk

Printed and bound in Great Britain
By In-House Printing, Huddersfield

Paperback ISBN 1 901679 72 1

Chapter 1	Early Days
Chapter 2	Second Gum Tree On The Left
Chapter 3	The White Man's Grave
Chapter 4	From New Delhi to Darjeeling
Chapter 5	Back to Africa
Chapter 6	Injun Country
Chapter 7	Filipino Frolics
Chapter 8	Other Far-flung Place
Chapter 9	On Reflection

ACKNOWLEDGEMENTS

The writer wishes to acknowledge the love and support of his family, both in experiencing and recalling the events described in this book. Without the encouragement and prompting of his daughters, Fiona, Louise and Lizzy, the book may never have been written.

He also thanks his many friends on all five continents and, in particular, his former colleagues and customers in the telecommunications industry, some of whom will no doubt recognise themselves in the text.

Thanks also go to the gentlemen of the Alderley Edge PROBUS for their forbearance in listening to extracts and for providing the confidence to go to publication. The anecdotes do not set out to ridicule anyone or any nation; they reflect observations and amusement as seen through the eyes of one curious Englishman.

CHAPTER 1
EARLY DAYS

Why on earth I should have developed a thirst for global travel is one of life's mysteries. Neither of my parents had ventured outside Great Britain, although the movement by a pharmaceutical company of certain managers, including my father, from their Nottingham headquarters to a new manufacturing plant at Airdrie in central Scotland did have a profound effect in extending their hitherto limited horizons.

For my dear old Mum, to whom a trip to the Lincolnshire coast had been a major expedition, visits to places such as Inverness and Oban must have been as exotic as travelling to Rio de Janeiro or Hong Kong. They were, as you might say, contented with their lot, a luxury which eludes so many of higher means and aspiration.

As a seven year old I had incurred my father's wrath, justifiably since we were still suffering the austerity of the Second World War, by purchasing, for the princely sum of two shillings, a book on life in Ceylon, Burma and India. When he had cooled down, and having observed my deep interest in the contents, Dad offered to buy me the full series of twelve, covering the entire British Empire, but only as he could afford it. Five Pounds a week was a frugal wage with five mouths to feed.

Previously the extent of my curiosity had been where the River Trent came from and where it went to below Nottingham. Now I was becoming aware of the mysteries that lay beyond. Philately inserted itself among the other hobbies of a normal young lad in the Forties: train spotting, cigarette cards, Meccano, roller-skating, cycling, cricket and football. My mind buzzed with wonder at where these multifarious scraps of perforated paper had started their journeys. Among them were names that have now been consigned to the history books. Who can remember Tannou Touva, Straits Settlements, Gold Coast and St.Pierre & Miquelon?

Geography had always captured my interest at school, even though it was restricted to two forty-five minutes periods per week. The primary effect of Scotland on my geographical education was to engender a passionate interest in hills and mountains. For this, much of my thanks must go to my old geography master, J. Harrison (Paddy) Maxwell. It was not so much Paddy's knowledge, which was never in doubt, as his enthusiasm that spurred me on. Indeed we had many a mischievous laugh at his expense as we roamed the quarries and mosses of North Lanarkshire in search of geological specimens.

You could present Paddy with any rock from gneiss to chalk and he would toss back his white-maned and bearded head and declare, without fear of contradiction, "Quartz, boy, definitely quartz!"

Initially, at the age of twelve, my focus was on contour maps and Paddy had a drawer full. I still have one old map which he gave me, The Edinburgh Geographical Institute's cloth backed coverage of South Northumberland, price Two Shillings. That would raise a few eyebrows amongst today's green belt protectors in the Tyneside area!

Many happy hours were spent in drawing lines from one

point to another and then plotting the vertical height against the distance between. By this simple but absorbing means it was possible to create an approximation of the panorama to be seen from any point covered by the Ordnance Survey. A careful transcription of the Campsie Fells as seen from Airdrie gave me sufficient satisfaction to feel that my efforts were not entirely futile.

Finally the day came when I set off from Kilsyth, rucksack on my back, to trek up the Campsies and see what the world looked like from up there. It was a modest ascent and very boggy but the view from the Meikle Bin on a clear spring day was awe inspiring. New shapes and new names were fed into my ravenous cranium: Ben Ime, Ben Laoigh, Stobinian, Stuc a Chroin, Ben Vorlich. The names flow on.

Next stop was Ben Ledi in the Trossachs, followed by the Cairngorms, the beautiful, majestic Cairngorms, without doubt the single most influential factor in my youth. It was there, high above the old Caledonian forests of Rothiemurchus, long before the advent of the noxious commercialisation of Strathspey, that I began to discover the self within myself. It was there that I started to come to terms with my conscience, where I developed philosophies on life which have hardly changed over fifty years. It was there that I realised that the time given to each of us to explore the infinite wonders of this world is itself short and finite.

I am not a deeply religious person. Subsequent travel has taken me amongst many of the world's religious groups and I find it difficult to devote myself to any one particular creed. There are good and bad, erudite and ignorant, leaders and followers in all beliefs. They cannot all be right. My dilemma is, does it really matter, if the heart and the mind are on the right course? I happen to have been born into a Church of England family. Am I duty bound therefore to accept without question the tenets of Canterbury?

I think not and I reject the accusations of blatant escapism and dangerous subjectivity levelled by certain sections of the Church at he who claims to feel closer to God when walking in the Yorkshire Dales than he does when sitting in a church. Such are my own feelings, first experienced on the high plateaux of the Cairngorms and repeated many times since. Non-denominational is a term with which I can live comfortably.

We were tough little devils at that time, some would say masochistic. Night after night under canvas in sub-zero temperatures was our idea of pleasure, waking up in our Black's Polar sleeping bags with frost on our eyebrows and crawling outside to find every source of water turned to ice, forcing our blistered feet into solid, frozen boots and baring our vitals to the cruel elements as we crouched over some wind lashed latrine.

Accommodation at Glenmore Lodge, the old lodge that is, now a Youth Hostel, was luxury indeed. Above all it had a drying room. Well do I remember the names of the rooms in that outpost of Paradise: Ryvoan, Braeriach, Ben Macdhui, Skoran Dhu and Bynack Mor amongst them. Ben The Hoose was the source of the most nourishing, fortifying porridge ever made, with salt and water, not milk and sugar, ye Sassenach loons.

One day, while returning with a party of Lanarkshire school children from Glenmore Lodge across the high wilderness between Ben Macdhui and Cairngorm, we ran into total whiteout conditions. Everything went white, the sky, the mist, the snow covered ground; there was no horizon, no definition at all. All securely roped together, we edged by map and compass across the plateau until there was a marginal respite in the weather. Almost immediately a white figure on skis swept up to us.

"If you see any of my men, tell them to get off the mountain," he screeched. "It's too dangerous for them to be out."

Puzzled, I asked, "Who are you?"

Back came the response, "Army commandos."

Agreeing to assist if we could, my party of fourteen year olds completed their mission safely and without a whimper.

On another occasion I was precariously perched on a ledge high in the North facing Coire an Lochan. I was leading a rope of three. It was dark and remarkably quiet, the rock was icy and I was perplexed as to my next move when a toffee paper drifted past, nearly landing on my nose. I peered up, dazzled by the bright sky above the black rock face. There, grinning back at me, was Mischief itself, a young urchin not unlike the ones I had led up there myself.

"Ee, 'e can't gerrup!" he informed his pal, both of them spread-eagled on their stomachs seeing who could land a toffee wrapper on my head first. Then they disappeared, summoned no doubt by a panic stricken guide who had spotted their perilous position on the edge of a black void. I never heard or saw them again.

After a brief and spectacularly unsuccessful period studying pharmacy at Glasgow University, I placed myself at Her Majesty's disposal in the Royal Corps of Signals. I was one of a minority in khaki to have enjoyed Catterick Camp in the Fifties, situated as it is adjacent to Swaledale and Wensleydale, with Richmond, a town full of historic character, as the main watering hole.

In December 1955, "Zambesi" was top of the hit-parade and was repeated *ad nauseam* on the juke-box in the bar of the Bishop's Blaize in Richmond's cobbled market place. Sadly this was the limit of local interest to most of the squaddies of the day. Little heed was paid to the more esoteric attractions lurking in the winding alleys, museums and ancient buildings of that splendid town. Booze was the god and oblivion was the objective.

Discipline was harsh; humour was dark but plentiful at Catterick. What else in an establishment where it was *de rigeur* that the top layer of coal in each bunker be painted white, where, during a drought, the grass was painted green and any stone protruding above the water line in the stream which bisected the camp had to be whitewashed. That was the Army of Blanco and Brasso; none of your stay-bright alloys or synthetic webbing in those days.

Never will I forget the panic when a piercing shriek aroused our barrack room one midnight to the plight of a damsel in serious distress. We were all aware that the IRA had been attacking mainland military targets such as the armoury at Arborfield Garrison. We were not yet trained soldiers and we knew it. Bravery amounted to peering nervously through the window into a black void. Nothing there, back to bed chaps, back into your chariots.

Clang, clang, clang.

"All fall in in front of the Regimental Office!"

No arguing this time, whatever the time of night, this was the Regimental Sergeant Major.

"Right, you lot, who heard or saw anything untoward during the night? Ashman?"

"Nothing, Sir."

"Brompton?"

"Nothing, Sir."

And so on down the line until one hapless sod inevitably blurted out, "She screamed, Sir, but by the time I had put on my trousers she had run away."

As he disappeared at double speed in the direction of the guard room, the rest of us learned that a sergeant major's daughter had been indecently assaulted fifty yards from our billet, the last in Kemmel Lines, on her way home across a field to married quarters.

The detainee was of course innocent, which he eventually established with considerable difficulty, but it did provide some mirth over the naiveté of raw youth pitched into the cauldron of military discipline. The decent side of us sympathised deeply with the SM's daughter but a regular chuckle was an essential to counter the great deprivations of service life at that time.

A good laugh at another rookie's expense occurred shortly afterwards on the assault course. An icy wind was shearing down from the Bellerby Moors; the rain was arrowing in at an angle of forty-five degrees. A hard-bitten sergeant from Wigan, who had drawn the short straw and knew it, and some thirty forlorn and soggy rookies were pitted against the quagmire which passed for Loos assault course. Some tried to pretend that it presented a worthy challenge. Grampian, Lakeland and Snowdonian peaks had been overcome in worse conditions. Cross-country runs could be quite exciting in adverse weather. Potholing was a doddle, the muddier the better. But to the majority it was a crass intrusion into their personal comfort.

Over the greasy cross poles we went, over the eight foot wall, under the cargo net. Splish-splosh, splish-splosh. The *pièce-de-resistance* however was a three feet diameter Stanton and Staveley pipe, some twenty yards in length and half filled with mud and water as sticky as treacle. Now, all squaddies, whatever their lack of rank or experience, know that a soldier's best friend is his rifle. Whatever else may suffer, the rifle must remain immaculate at all times. One's life and the lives of others may depend on it. Unfortunately someone forgot to tell Potter.

Potter was one of those unfortunates caught for National Service between graduation from university and their twenty-sixth birthday. An academic with an honours degree in engineering and very pleasant too, but physically illiterate and totally disorientated in a military training environment. In other words, a drill sergeant's dream.

As each man completed the course, he reported to the drill sergeant and fell into line. Eventually out came a forlorn brown sack, sodden from its helmet to its boots, excruciatingly cold and bearing the expression of a deeply aggrieved bloodhound. It took the sarge about five seconds to recognise the lump as Potter and a further nanosecond to realise the unimaginable.

"Soldier, where is your bondook?"

"I'm sorry Sergeant, I must have dropped it in the pipe."

"Well get back in the bloody pipe and find it!"

Down went Potter, on hands and knees into the end of the pipe from which he had recently emerged. After three feet he came head to head with the next heap of misery picking its way through the slime.

"F--- off Potter!!!", came the cry from within.

Needing no second invitation, the sergeant grabbed Potter's gaiters and yanked. Splosh! Down he went, face in the mud as he was dragged unceremoniously out.

"Get back to the other end, your bloody earthworm!"

Off staggered the bedraggled Potter, bereft of any shred of pride or thought by this time. Tap, tap, tap went the sergeant's right boot, twenty years of drilling all manner of idiots and misfits having already told him what was to ensue.

Out from the pipe came the next man, his own rifle, still in pristine condition, held carefully above the water line in one hand and Potter's, looking for all the world like an abandoned garden hoe, in the other.

"Found this in the mud Sergeant." he said, snapping to attention.

"Thanks lad, fall in."

After three others, and what seemed like an eternity, the bedraggled Potter emerged, shaking partly from the numbing cold, but more so from absolute terror.

"Well?" queried the sergeant quietly and almost politely.

"It's n-n-not there Sergeant, it must have f-f-floated away."

What followed was like Hiroshima and Nagasaki rolled into one.

"Stand still soldier! Think you're on a bloody fly-past? Damaging War Department property, violating Queen's Regulations. That's for starters, you pathetic excuse for a seaside donkey. Report to the Guard Room and wait there for me."

There and then we would have given short odds on Potter heading for a glasshouse at Colchester or Shepton Mallet.

As for the rest of us, our own discomfiture was soon set aside as we stood under the steaming showers in full kit, enough mud flowing from our bodies to dam the Nile. Again it was a case of having a good laugh at some other unfortunate's expense, while deep down feeling a great deal of sympathy for him. There but for the Grace of God!

Such was military training.

Training does not last for ever, thank Heaven, and life on a working unit is an entirely different kettle of fish. I was overjoyed when I received my posting as a fully-fledged Electronic Technician Grade X3. Singapore. The name conjured up evocative images. But, while I was in transit at the aptly sounding Saighton Camp at Chester, an inconsiderate colonel in Cairo decided to block the Suez Canal. Troops were transported by ship in those days. As a result only half of the Singapore draft made it, via the Cape of Good Hope. The other half were scuttled off to Germany. I wound up in Rheindahlen, close to Moenchen Gladbach. However all was not doom and gloom. I found West Germany in the late fifties to be a most hospitable and interesting country.

In working a three way shift system at the Rhine Army headquarters, I was blessed with an abundance of quality spare time, midweek daytime when most others were working. By putting this to good effect it was possible to explore on foot many of the villages and rural tracks lying between Aachen, Rheindahlen and the Dutch border. In Germany, the Neanderthal Valley and the Drachenfels Mountains were comfortably within reach, while to the South West lay the Belgian Ardennes.

Away breaks in Holland were a delight, sometimes in Roermond or Venlo but usually in Nijmegen, home of the famous Vierdaagse. The Vierdaagse was an annual event to commemorate the relief of Nijmegen at the end of the Second World War. It comprised a series of marches over different routes in the Nijmegen-Arnhem area on four successive days. Our schedule, designed for military contingents, required us to march thirty miles on each day. The run up to this entailed several weeks of gruelling training on the Wegberg Ring in Germany, not all the blistered feet making it to Holland.

The rigours of the preparation were well worth it. The poignancy of the occasion was evident to all of us as we marched over the terrain on which so many heroic wartime deeds had been performed. Cheering crowds at every point along the route made the marches themselves a pleasure that we did not want to end. Some of the older people were weeping as memories no doubt flooded back. I will never forget the beaming faces of the little children as we carried them aloft through their respective villages.

It was while relaxing in Nijmegen after the third day's march that I met Tini, a delightful girl from Oss in Noord Brabant. Not speaking each other's language was no barrier to our enjoyment of the local *pannekoeken*. We chattered and laughed in smatterings of English, French, German and Dutch and soon realised that the desire to meet again was mutual.

The fourth day was very special. All military contingents were required to stop on the outskirts of Nijmegen and to change into best battledress before marching formally into town. As our unit approached the main grandstand, erected for the VIPs to witness the taking of the salute by the Supreme Allied Commander, I was confronted by Tini, her arms full of flowers, her smile beaming from ear to ear!

"By the right, eyes right."

With thirty pairs of eyes trained on the SAC, I feared for Tini's safety and so, without hesitation, swept her into my arms, threw up my salute and marched past General Norstad in the grandest of style. On receiving the "Eyes front," I lowered her to the ground, patted her gently on her pretty little posterior and shooed her back into the watching crowd.

It was only when our unit had received the order to fall out, beyond the public view, that I worried about what had occurred. Fortunately, just before our unit commander could express his feelings on the subject, a despatch rider screeched to a halt with a message for the soldier who had borne the young lady aloft.

It read, "Well carried off! - Norstad."

"Phew!" gasped I.

"The Amstels are on you, Lofty," went up the cry.

It was a pleasure. The flowers were donated to a very grateful sergeant who had overlooked his wedding anniversary. The Lieutenant pocketed the note for *his* memoirs.

One of the highlights of my service life was the periodical courier duty, carrying high security despatches by train from Rheindahlen to Degendorf, a small Intelligence outpost near Rosenheim, close to the Austrian border. This presented the opportunity to venture into the local mountains, Wildenkaiser, the Wendelstein and the Riesenkopf Pinnacle among them. It was on one of these courier trips that I passed through Munich on the day following the tragic Manchester United air disaster. In the pall of smoke on the station platform as we awaited our departure, one could physically feel the grief in the air.

Service life is full of surprises. So it was one morning when a notice appeared on the Order Office notice-board requesting the names of anyone with mountaineering or skiing experience. Ignoring the first commandment of service life, that is, never volunteer for anything, I appended my number, rank and name.

Three weeks later I was informed that I was to be despatched to St. Johann in Tyrol with a number of other lucky devils from across BAOR to undergo three weeks of Army ski training. No uniforms, for Austria was a neutral country, no rank, a first-class hotel at the base of the Kitzbueheler Horn, what more could one ask for? Our *langlauf* instructor was the former world champion, Willi "shtick ze bo-bo in" Noikl.

The weather was idyllic throughout. How could we fail? The high spot of the course was a descent of the Hannenkahm, a few days after the local hero Toni Seiler had made it look so easy in the world downhill championships.

"Easy," says the man. If I skied every day from now to Doomsday I could not master the Mousetrap on that particular run!

Later that year, 1958, came the inevitable return to civilian life. In spite of the undoubted attractions of service life, the camaraderie, the opportunities for sport and adventure, the involvement in a key branch of service communications and, believe it or not, the independence, I knew in my heart of hearts that I was not cut out to be a Field Marshal.

Readjusting to the civilian world is not easy when you have been fed, clothed, housed and paid by the Crown for three years. With some effort it was accomplished. Laboratory work in Motherwell and then in Edinburgh was combined with a very pleasant social life and some serious assaults on a succession of Scottish peaks.

During this period I was called on by Glasgow Corporation to guide a party of foreign visitors to the top of Ben Lomond. The appointed Saturday was definitely a day for staying indoors. The drizzle was incessant; the wind was cold and raw and a dank swirling mist cut visibility to a few yards. Still my motley crew of Europeans were enthusiastically in favour of an ascent and I had never yet been deterred by the weather, so off we set.

As the party strung out it soon became clear that things could easily get out of control. I halted the leaders until the tail-enders caught up and explained the dangers of becoming separated, suggesting that they split into two groups and never lost contact with their group. Meantime I shot up and down between the groups to check on their progress and give some encouragement. I assumed they were all townies and totally devoid of any mountain craft.

When we were all safely atop the Ben the clouds miraculously parted to reveal a magnificent view of Loch Lomond and the Trossachs. As we settled down for a well earned snack a serious little fellow in a tartan tammy sat beside me and informed me, "You know, I am Austrian, I am a professional mountain guide in Austria. I did not tell you this before because you are doing very well without my interference."

That I thought was modesty itself and I thanked him self-consciously before steering the unified party down once more into murk and misery.

Participation in mountain rescue was an inevitable activity, often rewarding, sometimes despairing as lives were lost. My worst moment came in a one hundred and twenty feet fall from Cousin's Buttress on the north-east face of Ben Nevis. The fall was bad enough; the tragic sight of the young Aberdeen student I had gone to rescue will stay with me for the rest of my days.

A career in Scotland was a tough assignment for an

ambitious young man in the early Sixties. What work there was, was poorly remunerated when compared to the lavish salaries being paid South of the Border. Like many of my peers, I took the carrot and, in March 1962, headed for the English Midlands. A new career in telecommunications loomed and very satisfying it was to prove as I remained with the same company for the next thirty-four years.

Life took on a new dimension in 1963 when I fell hook, line and sinker for a beautiful young lady who was to become my wife and mother of two wonderful daughters.

It was clear to me already, from experiences in the Army, that the world outside Britain was full of little surprises. It did not surprise me therefore that I was soon on the wrong end of a laugh on our first Continental holiday. We had checked in at a hotel resembling a mediaeval castle in Bellinzona in the Italian speaking South of Switzerland. It was a balmy evening. The whole town was bathed in a fiery glow from the setting sun and it was dusty. On retiring to our room I noticed a pair of men's shoes outside the adjacent bedroom door.

"Aha!" I said, glancing down at my own ochre coated footwear, "a shoe cleaning service."

Thinking no more of it, I left my shoes in the corridor and went to bed.

Emerging next morning, expecting to find a lustrous pair of Grensons awaiting me, I was dismayed to see my dust covered shoes still very much covered in dust, but with a note inside. Neither I nor my wife, who knew a smattering of Italian, could make head or tail of the message scrawled thereon.

It wasn't until we reached Milan later in the day that I related the tale and showed the note to an English speaking Italian. He immediately curled up in laughter and retold the story to a couple of friends who also convulsed. Leaving a client's shoes in the corridor was apparently a professional lady's way of notifying anyone whom it may concern that she was engaged therein. On seeing my size elevens alongside those of her client, she wondered who was muscling in on her manor.

I worked diligently through the sixties, initially as a draughtsman and later as an equipment design engineer, establishing the foundations of family life. Our first daughter, Fiona, was born in 1964, a beautiful little bundle of love to be sure.

Every year we somehow managed a holiday in Dorset, Devon or Cornwall. Fiona was finding her feet in 1967 when we made for Looe. I will always remember the day of arrival. All the new guests, in true English fashion, sat around feeling self-conscious and gazing at the carpet. The silence was deafening until Fiona broke it with devastating effect.

"Daddy, move your spout over so that I can sit down."

All were friends thereafter.

At about the same time Fiona moved from a cot into her own bed. On the first night I was sleeping soundly when I was awoken by a determined little fist pummelling my forehead.

Jerking up in the pitch darkness, I called out, "What's going on?"

The reply came from low down to my left where a little

voice enquired in a whisper, "Daddy, if I flush the toilet, will it wake you up?"

What can one say?

The following year saw the arrival of our second daughter, Louise. Upon her emergence the family doctor ventured, "Not bad for a first attempt."

On being informed that it was our second he reviewed his initial appraisal and rebuked, "In that case it is pathetic!"

May I correct him. She was gorgeous and, like her sister, still is.

In 1969, two further major events occurred in my life. Firstly, in March, my father succumbed to carcinoma of the pancreas. Suddenly I felt very vulnerable without the indestructible pillar on whom I had leant for support and advice throughout my life hitherto.

Secondly, I spoke to my Engineering Manager about the benefits of spending a period on a working site, away from the design office, in order to gain an appreciation of the problems faced by the customer in operating and maintaining equipment which I had designed. A month on a working radio station in England was what I had in mind, most likely with what was then the British Post Office, later to become BT. The outcome was totally unexpected.

"Ah!" gasped the Installation and Commissioning Manager. "Just the chap I need. How do you fancy a couple of months in Australia? Home for Christmas, guaranteed."

Another of life's great myths was about to explode - an Englishman's word is his bond.

I duly discussed the pros and cons with my wife, the

career benefits, the financial leg-up, the impositions and disruption of family life. Neither of us had been beyond San Marino; Australia seemed as remote as Mars. But we agreed that it was a cross-roads, an opportunity which, once refused, might not recur and very soon I found myself on a commissioning course along with another two dozen aspirants.

The company had recently suffered considerable adverse criticism over the poor performance of its field staff on a contract in Nova Scotia and consequently decided to make the selection for Australia competitive. Fortunately for me, radio technology was at that time about to enter a new era. The industry had been totally reliant on thermionic valves throughout its earlier history; the Perth - Adelaide microwave system was to be the first fully solid-state long-haul telecommunications system in the world. Transistors and integrated circuits were in. This had the effect of providing a level playing field for all on our training course and allowed me to qualify whereas otherwise I would have been at a considerable disadvantage in competing with established radio engineers.

Having duly graduated, I said my family farewells and set off for Heathrow.

Chapter 2
Second Gum Tree On The Left

The long-haul jets of 1969 could not compare in range and capacity with those of today. London - Rome - Karachi - Bangkok - Hong Kong on a Boeing 707 operated by BOAC made up the first leg. I wrote on a post-card to my family that everyone should have the opportunity to visit Hong Kong at least once in their lifetime. What a cultural shock to anyone who had never been beyond Europe!

Buzz, buzz, buzz, twenty-four hours a day, non-stop and all the time that unmistakable aroma of Oriental cooking permeating the humid tropical air. Kowloon in the evening, surrounded by a thousand Susie Wongs, rickshaws plying to and fro, Hawaiian and Chinese music floating from every other doorway, these are first time experiences one does not forget. I graciously declined the invitation of Pamela Fung, my hotel desk supervisor, to a conducted tour of the city by night. Perhaps I was a little hasty.

My arrival in Australia was quite disconcerting. Having endured the indignity of being sprayed with disinfectant in the aircraft prior to disembarking, I discovered that one of my suitcases had taken a terrific battering *en route* from Hong Kong, resulting in my first hour at Kingsford Smith Airport being spent in the company of a very sympathetic and conscientious baggage handler from Japan Air Lines.

Eventually boarding an Ansett-Ana flight for Adelaide, I politely asked a statuesque, blonde flight hostess whether they had any reading matter on board.

"Si'down, Pom, and speak when yer bladdy spoken to!"

I had arrived.

To complete my day, none of my baggage arrived at Adelaide on that flight. I was told that it had gone to Wagga Wagga and thought this was some form of Aussie joke, to be practised on every first time arrival from Mother England. But it turned out to be true. They recovered well; it was delivered to my hotel within three hours of my arrival there.

Adelaide is a very civilised city renowned for its plethora of churches and good restaurants. I would like to have spent longer there. However, after one business meeting, an afternoon in front of the television set watching Richmond and Sturt kick chunks out of each other in the Aussie Rules cup final and a fine barbecue with some English friends beside the Murray River, it was time to become airborne once more, destination Perth.

Now, Western Australia is quite different from South Australia and so are its people. Western Australia is roughly the same size as India, but for every fifteen Western Australians there are ten thousand Indians. Aborigines make up just over one percent of the population of one point five million. Most of the population are city dwellers, which leaves a heck of a lot of space for the remainder.

Tough and independent, when they take to you Western Australians rank with the finest friends a man can have. When they are not friendly, duck! Over the next few months I was to meet all types.

The desk-bound colleague back in England who had prepared the list of clothing items necessary for this job had included snake boots and pith helmet. Can you imagine the effect on a hairy backed Aussie of a white skinned Pommy emerging in such attire? Needless to say we disregarded his advice.

The Australian Post Office guy who met me off the train at Northam was a laid back, lived in looking individual if ever there was one.

"Bruce," he dropped out as if rationed to one word per conversation.

Would you believe it, the first real Aussie I meet is named Bruce? I had the same defensive feeling that I did about Wagga Wagga.

"Wanna roll-up?" asked Bruce, spitting onto a tatty piece of paper before sticking it around some fierce looking shag.

"Thanks, Bruce. If you don't mind, I'll stick to my Dunhills."

"Up you for the bleeding rent!" was the immediate riposte.

My new friend turned out to be like that all the time. No malice, just a very earthy growl. He never took offence, just repaid any dig with interest.

On the evening of my arrival in Northam, the town was deserted. An earthquake measuring 6.8 on the Richter scale had struck, centred on Meckering, a small wheat-belt town down the road. Aussies don't normally need any excuse to have a drink. Now that they had one they were too terrified to go out lest the earth broke open again and swallowed them. Earthquakes were hitherto unknown in those parts and no one knew quite what to make of the situation.

Sixty in-line stations had to be installed and commissioned between Perth and Adelaide. This worked out at one every twenty-five miles approximately, most of them out in the deep donga, but with a few handily sited in or near to strategic towns. The first town encountered was Merredin. We were accommodated in huge two man caravans which we hauled along with Dodge trucks. Merredin provided the opportunity to stock up the freezer with steak, steak and more steak. We ate fried steak and eggs for breakfast, grilled steak and chips for lunch and braised steak with whatever was available for dinner. Every day! Mad cow disease had not yet been discovered.

Life in the caravans was tough but they were well equipped and spacious. When in towns, it was possible to use communal showers and eat at whatever restaurants were available. Merredin was one such place, as were Southern Cross and Kalgoorlie. Out in the bush however, one had to be much more self-reliant, up at the sparrow's fart, to be at work by 8 a.m., with breakfast, laundry and ablutions in between.

The shower comprised a tarpaulin canopy at the rear of the van which had to be filled with cold water from jerry-cans. No such thing as cold water in the Australian bush, you might think. I tell you, it's all relative. It felt cold to me when the old release cord was pulled. It certainly woke one up.

A good breakfast was essential to face the long day ahead and we always brought the cooker into play. Anyway the steaks were too tempting and diets were not necessary, gangling beanpoles that we were.

Laundering had to be done at some point and early morning was the best time, to allow for drying in the ever present sun. Half an hour and the clothes were as stiff as a board. No one had told me that whites and coloureds don't mix. Armed with a cold water soap powder I threw everything in together and spent the rest of my time wandering across Australia in the most delicious flamingo pink underwear and sports shirts. After the first wash it did not really matter, the dye had been cast, to coin a phrase.

Ironing was a luxury which could have been readily dispensed with, there being no sartorial elegance in the bush. I had, however, heeded the words of an old soldier buddy in Germany who had spent much of his service time under canvas in Kenya, Nigeria, Borneo and Malaya.

"Bloody good thing, ironing," he had often said as he pressed his battledress, "kills off all those guinea worms and tumbu flies and the like that bore in and crawl under your skin."

As there seemed to be infinite scope for such parasites where we were, I ironed everything, even my pink shreddies.

Lunch was always welcome, although stepping from the air-conditioned equipment room into the outdoor furnace was something of a deterrent and always came as a shock to the system. Evenings were fine in the towns, but out in the sticks, after dinner and letter writing, it was usually preferable to go back into the station and carry on working. You can get carried away with testing when there are no outside disturbances and often we would keep going until one or two o'clock in the morning. We were aware that the sooner we finished, the sooner we would be home and apart from that, the overtime pay was always welcome.

We were paid on a tax free basis, all salaries going into the National Bank of Ireland in Dublin. Severe cash flow problems arose when the bank went on strike for several weeks in 1970. I telephoned them at considerable expense and had a pleasant ten minute conversation with a seemingly very helpful chap, until he told me that he was only the watchman and no permanent staff were available. One of my colleagues wrote to Dublin and received a reply which stated, and you've got to believe this, "Should you fail to receive this correspondence, please notify us without delay."

We had to exercise some care in Merredin as one of our Installation Engineers had earlier taken the canopy off the only petrol station, not yet having become accustomed to the huge hulk which he was towing. The approach of any Dodge towed caravan was treated with utmost suspicion.

The radio station names had been derived on an arbitrary basis by the initial surveying team. Some were intriguing sounding aboriginal names such as Oomblegabby and Nunjikompita, others were named after the nearest local landmark of any significance One of the latter was Tank Hill which lay adjacent to the concrete lined, steel water pipeline which stretched some three hundred and fifty miles from Mundaring Weir, in the Darling Ranges behind Perth to Kalgoorlie, and then beyond into the Great Victoria Desert.

My caravan partner at that stage was a rangy Liverpudlian with a crush on Barbra Streisand and a masochistic sense of humour. Once when I crashed my head on the joist above the caravan door and went feet first on my back down the access steps, he looked on disdainfully, commenting, "That looked exciting Blue, can I have a go?"

There were times when he drove me to distraction, none more so than the night when he lumbered round the caravan in total darkness, crashing into every fixed object and finally disappearing out of the door. I glanced at my watch. 11.30 p.m. No doubt gone for a pee. I dozed off to sleep.

When I awoke it was 1.15 a.m. No sound of the usual grunts and snores, so I shone my torch across to the other bed. Empty.

Strange, a pee does not take two hours and there is nowhere else to go at Tank Hill. Donning my boots and a pair of slacks I went out into the balmy night air. I called his name, as loud as I could, for no one else would hear. Silence. I shone my torch around and walked to all corners of the compound. Nothing. Good God, we had heard stories of dingoes and we had seen some formidable looking brown snakes and red back spiders. What if.......?

I was now by the three and a half feet diameter water pipe which lay in a broad trench so that half of the pipe was below ground level. In the distance, as I looked along the pipe, I could see a pin prick of light. Must be a bush homestead, I thought. Then it flashed. I was sure it flashed. Yes, there it was again. I climbed aboard my Dodge and headed off on the sandy track beside the pipe towards the light. There was no way of telling how far away it was.

Gradually it grew brighter until I was able to discern that it was not one light but two. Yes, headlights.

I found Big Jim some two miles from the compound looking mightily relieved to see me, his truck buried up to the axles in sand.

"What the flaming Ada are you doing here?" was the obvious question.

"Sorry, Blue, I felt like a comfortable crap and this was the first place I came to where I could sit back and lean against the pipe with a gap in the trench below me. I tried to turn the truck round and got stuck in the sand."

I was speechless. Given the catalogue of nocturnal nasties that frequent the Australian outback, anyone who bares his backside at two in the morning must be twice round the hat rack. With some difficulty we hauled his Dodge out of the soft sand and onto the pipe-side track.

As we crawled back into bed, both thoroughly knackered, a guilty voice ventured, "You know, Blue, the stars are really brilliant out here in the bush."

I farted and disappeared into a deep dreamless sleep.

At Number Seven Tank, just beyond the small town of Southern Cross, I was introduced to the native skill of boomerang manufacture. In the absence of any suitable mulga trees, Adrian, my instructor, carved up a handy packing crate with remarkable aplomb. The first product had a sharp bend and fulfilled all my notions of what a boomerang should look like.

"Naa," he said with disdain, "that's what you get in the tourist shops down in Perth. A plaything, no self respecting Abo would be seen holding that."

He then produced a much straighter implement with an aerodynamically fashioned leading edge of which Boeing would have been proud.

"That's a woomerbanger!" he proclaimed proudly, "she's a beaut, meant to kill, not to fly round in bloody circles all day."

With that he drew back a mighty arm, cast it forward, cocking his wrist at the point of release and grunted.

"Aaaagh!"

He was still grunting when the blessed thing came round half circle at twice the speed at which he had launched it, narrowly missed us both and went whoosh, whoosh, whoosh, whoosh smash, through the windscreen of my Dodge.

It was at Number Seven Tank that I had my first close brush with a snake. I had seen plenty before, especially basking on the rocks at Tammin, the station before Merredin, but not at such close quarters. Stepping down from the caravan, I was hailed by Big Jim.

"See what you just stepped over, Blue?"

I turned round to see a fiendish looking brown snake, which must have been all of seven feet long, lapping the drips from the sink waste pipe below the van. It took frequent breaks from its drinking to eye me up before coiling up and nodding off. We went nowhere near the van until it had disappeared. The steps were never used again for descending from the van. Jonathan Edwards would have been amused by our alighting technique.

Finlayson was an interesting station on which to work. The local watering hole was the Denver City Hotel at the

Old Camp, Coolgardie. Why they call it the ghost town is not difficult to fathom out. The population in the cemetery is bigger than that of the town. In these days, when water comes on tap, it is impossible to comprehend the hardships which the early prospectors must have endured. Even more so those endured by the trans-continental explorers such as Ernest Giles whose grave and monument are there in Coolgardie.

The bar in the Denver City was one of the bleakest I have encountered anywhere, a bare stone wall providing the backdrop. This, I was reliably informed, was to minimise the repair costs occasioned by the local womenfolk, whose practice it was to hurl the last of their empty glasses at the wall before staggering home.

The stories reaching us from further up the route were at first beyond credibility. By now some of them were seemingly possible. It was rumoured that one group had met a party of Melbourne models who had decided to forego the catwalk for a trip around the perimeter of Australia. Meeting up far beyond the limits of civilisation, there had been a natural empathy which had developed into more permanent relationships. These girls were known as the tea-ladies and had taken a temporary leave from their main objective to take up residence in the caravans of our advance party. They were to spend several months accompanying the team, some of the relationships turning out to be more permanent than was envisaged at that time.

Tea-ladies were certainly not on my mind as I was testing Emu Hill, the last station before Kalgoorlie. I was in agony with piles. The searing heat only made matters worse and there was a constant stream of sweat running down my back and between the cheeks of my backside. There was no option but to visit a doctor in Kalgoorlie. On examination, he immediately transferred me to the local infirmary where I was planted into a ward with five other sufferers. Each thought it was his birthday to have an agony contorted, bed-ridden Pommy, incapable of escape, as his room victim.

What I said I don't know but, after one day and night, the ribbing subsided and friendship grew. There was a retired gold miner in the opposite corner with ulcerated legs that looked as though they had stood before a Nigerian firing squad.

"Christ, Lofty, I feel sorry for you. Must be bloody agony," he sympathised, he who looked as if he had been through two world wars and would never walk again.

Those old-timers ran the poor nurses ragged and the nurses took it all in good part, often giving as good as they got. There was one tough looking cookie who knew better than all the others how to look after herself. It was she who approached my bed one evening, drew the screen and blurted menacingly, "Jeez, Pom, am I going to enjoy this!"

I was defenceless, legs trussed up round my ears to let the ice packs do their work.

"Aaaaagh!" was all I could muster as she thrust some cigar shaped object into my back passage.

"Bitch!"

"Ne'er mind, Pom, have you crawling out of here in no time."

Three weeks passed before my chance for revenge

arrived. I spotted Sharlene, the nurse, in the bar of the Palace Hotel with one of her colleagues.

"Hi, buy you a drink?" I asked.

I got her so drunk that I had to deliver her by pick-a-back to the hospital residential quarters. I just hoped that her hangover matched the pain in my arse.

Drinking is the national sport in Oz. On the Goldfields it is the religion. Fighting is the inevitable sequel. For a Pom it is very definitely a danger zone and one needs a clear head at all times. We developed a routine of drinking plenty but over a long period.

I spent several weeks in Kalgoorlie, during which time I became quite fond of the place and learned how to survive there. That Aussies are big drinkers is no myth, trouble is they can't hold it. As a result closing time at Kalgoorlie's bars was outrageously early.

We found a cunning way to circumnavigate this problem. By staking out a claim for mineral rights over some unwanted, barren area of the bush, well away from the genuine gold and nickel deposits which had all been gobbled up by Western Mining, one could, for the princely sum of five shillings, obtain a certificate from Kalgoorlie Town Hall granting mining rights over the staked area. Armed with this seemingly spurious piece of parchment, one could then descend on a certain hostelry in the neighbouring town of Boulder, where mine host was required, under the terms of his licence, to keep his bar open until the last miner had left the premises. Can you imagine the expression on the face of a shagged out, sleep starved Aussie bar owner, frustrated by a group of thirsty

Poms still drinking at four in the morning?

It was during my stint in Kalgoorlie that the price of Poseidon mining shares climbed off the scale. Grandmothers were tearing up floorboards to uncover fortunes in forgotten stock. Up, up and up they went. Poseidon fever hit Kalgoorlie. Masses congregated outside the stockbrokers' windows to monitor the upward movement. Nobody wanted to sell and miss the possibility of an even higher bonanza. However, what goes up usually comes down again and, in the case of Poseidon, these previously near worthless shares climbed over several days to astronomical heights and then fell over a cliff within minutes. Oh dear, dear, dear. The frenzy had to be witnessed to be believed. That there were suicides was no surprise. Many sorrows were drowned in Kal's bars that night and for several days and nights afterwards.

One of the stranger sides of Kalgoorlie was Hay Street. I saw the local chief of police deny on state television in Perth that Hay Street existed. Quite right, Sir. Neither it did. The name sign called it Barrack Street, but to the world and his friend it has always been known as Hay Street. It was an unpretentious little thoroughfare, some two hundred yards long, bordered on both sides by small shanty like knocking shops. Here a collection of god-forsaken looking women, bored out of their minds, plied their wretched trade from behind barred, glassless windows resembling rabbit hutches.

In a town where a large majority of the population were single men who grovelled underground for long hours and emerged with spectacular wage packets, Hay Street was seen as a safety valve which afforded considerable protection to the respectable ladies of the community. It also served the needs of some of our field staff.

We had two installers who worked together as a team. They were always arguing, but woe betide the man who tried to separate them. One Saturday evening, Monty, a veteran of the Malayan hostilities, in which he had been severely wounded and copped a packet of Lavender Rose into the bargain, decided it was time for a break. Making sure that Fred, his partner, had a good grasp of what needed to be done in his absence on the installation front, Monty set off for town, nominally to have a beer. He duly returned, rosy faced and smiling.

"Lovely," he said, "off you go son, your turn."

Off went Fred in the same direction and returned after an hour.

Quietly they worked on, then, "Had a remarkable experience in town." said Fred.

"Bedded this fabulous bird in Hay Street. We really hit it off. Said she loved me and wants to see me again. I think she meant it."

Pause.

"Was she big built, red haired and Hungarian?" asked Monty.

"Yes, how the hell did you know?"

"I had her about twenty minutes before you did."

Fred's reaction was furious.

"You swine!" he shouted, hurling himself at Monty. "Everything I do, you have to screw it up."

Yes, quite literally, the rest of us thought.

The route turned due south at Kalgoorlie, heading towards Norseman. There were three stations in between, one of which was Mount Edwards at Widgiemooltha. There were four telephones, a post office and a small inn at Widgie. It was a refreshing change after the wild west hurly-burly of Kalgoorlie. But it had its moments too.

Big Jim and Barry, an Ulsterman with eyes that oscillated at fifty cycles per second, were already in town. On my first evening there we decided that, for a change, we would go for a drink. The hotel had a very pleasant beer garden accessed through a dainty little wicket gate. As Barry opened the gate, a young couple approached from the garden. Ever the gentleman, Barry held the gate open and nodded to the pretty young lady.

"After you, Ma'am," he said in his soft Belfast lilt.

"You trying to get off with my sheila, you four-eyed Irish git?" was the boyfriend's response as he headbutted Barry, smashing his spectacles and dropping him to the deck.

Barry soon recovered but revised his thoughts on civility and when to apply it in Australia.

While testing Mount Edwards Barry came out with one of those violations of the English language which only an Irishman can. When asked whether a precise frequency requested by Kalgoorlie was being correctly transmitted, he replied, "It's approximately spot on."

It was also in Widgie that Big Jim and Barry decided to do some night walking.

"Oh, no! Not again," I groaned.

Having ventured a short distance into the bush, they stopped and looked around into the blackness of the encircling gum trees.

"Say, Jim, how do we know which way we have come?"

"Don't worry, Blue," replied Jim.

Everyone was Blue to Big Jim. It sounded very Australian, although I only ever heard Australians apply the name to fellows with ginger hair.

"I can tell by the stars. It's a clear night and all we have to do is pick out Sirius. It sits due North."

"Which one is Sirius?" asked a bemused Barry.

Jim scoured the brilliant night sky. After eliminating all other possibilities he announced, "It's directly over our heads."

As they looked around all they could see were gum trees stretching away in every direction.

"Sorry, Blue, we've got a problem."

They knew that, if they chose the wrong line, they could walk for hundreds of miles without finding anything other than more gum trees. They fell silent and listened.

Chug, chug, chug.

It was the unmistakable throb of a donkey engine that they heard. Off they went towards it, only to be confronted after a few hundred yards by a towering cliff rising out of the eucalyptus. They were off course by one hundred and eighty degrees, the sound rebounding from the cliff. Climbing the crag offered some hope. As they rose they again heard the chug of the donk and, in the same direction, saw the lights of civilisation. What they did not realise was that the lights were those of Kambalda, twenty-three miles away.

Heading off in that direction they eventually came to a

fence wire. Taking a gamble on which way to proceed they were startled by the barking of a very efficient and diligent sounding guard dog. This was soon followed by the snarling of a highly excited cockie emerging from his homestead.

"Who's there, what d'yer want yer bloody dingoes?"

Not a man to be trifled with as he probably had a loaded and cocked rifle to hand.

"Sorry, friend, we're lost. Trying to find the way to Widgiemooltha," ventured Jim.

"Well come out here with yer bloody hands up and I'll show yer the bloody way."

Close call but they made it back. Moral, avoid Big Jim at night.

It was at the next station, Pioneer, that I first got word from Barry that going home for Christmas was a forlorn dream.

"Come on, Barry, that's not funny," I growled.

"It's true, I got word over the radio from Kal this morning," he said apologetically.

My spirits sank to my boots. I was pissed off for my own sake at being misled by the company, but I was furious that my family back home should miss out when all along they had been assured that Daddy would be home for Christmas.

Next day, I completed Pioneer pre-commissioning and drove down to Norseman. It reminded me of what I thought a cowboy town in Wyoming would have looked like in the nineteenth century. There I waited for the Deputy Field Manager who, I was told, would be hitting town that morning. Eventually he arrived and, spotting me from the corner of his eye, crept off in the opposite direction as if inspecting the unbelievably boring displays in the windows of the few shops in the main street.

We had a right ding dong. I had been assured that I would be going home prior to Christmas.

"Ah, yes, but the job is behind schedule and everyone has to stay until completion to avoid penalties. The order is from UK, not Perth. Jobs cannot be guaranteed for anyone who goes home prematurely."

I knew it wasn't Ray's fault but I had to vent my spleen on someone in authority and he was the only manager available. We got on fine after that and were to remain good friends to this day.

That off my chest, I made my way into the bar of the Norseman Hotel. I had been forewarned that the local Australian Post Office man was one Davie Parsons and that he hated Poms and drank like a fish.

"Give him a wide berth," was the advice received in Kalgoorlie.

"Not on your Nelly! Let's meet this antipodean ogre," thought I.

"Is Davie Parsons here?" I enquired nervously.

"No mate, he drinks at the other place."

I made my way along the dusty road to the Railway Hotel. By the time I reached this hostelry my nerves had disappeared. It was Saturday noon and the half of Norseman males who were not in the Norseman Hotel were noisily gulping and shouting to each other at the bar of the Railway.

I stood at the door and bawled, "Who is Davie Parsons?" Silence fell like a guillotine.

"Who the fuck wants him?" drawled a solitary voice.

I announced myself.

"What does he fucking want him for?"

"To drink him under the fucking table," I replied.

The crowd parted, beer slurped everywhere and out of the throng stepped a crag of a man with whom I was to become very friendly, but not yet.

"Right, yer Pommy bastard, you're on!" chortled Parsons with relish.

"Jugs?" he suggested.

"Jugs it is," I agreed.

Intrigued that a wimp of a Pommy bastard dare challenge a local drinking legend, the crowd swarmed round the table that had been cleared for the confrontation. The first two jugs, one each, disappeared in an instant. Four more quickly followed them. Even though light headed myself, I began to detect a slur in Parsons' patois. I guess he'd had a head start on me before my arrival. Gradually my head spun more and more. I do not remember passing out, but I do remember coming to, lying on the floor with Parsons unconscious beside me.

The crowd had reverted to the bar. Climbing unsteadily to my chair, I called for two more jugs of Swannie

"Coming, yer Pommy bastard," came the startled reply.

Jug in hand and with the gallery regrouped, I rolled the limp torso over with my foot.

"Uuugh. What the hell's going on?" it groaned.

"C'mon Parsons," I somehow babbled out and, heaving

my new jug to my lips, I continued, "giving up already, you bloody sand groper?"

At that instant everything changed. The locals cheered, Parsons stretched up his hand in despair and conceded defeat. I was accepted. After that none of our lads had any trouble with Davie and his crew. We all got on famously together, on and off the job.

My first night at the Railway was somewhat restless. I had quaffed far too much lager and had a head like thunder. Moreover I was not too sure about the security of the hotel, so I locked my bedroom door.

Crash!

"Aw shit, who's in there?" screamed a female voice.

"Some bloody Pom who thinks he's going to get raped," squawked another.

It was the arrival of the early morning chamber maids, serving, believe it or not, tea in bed.

I soon discovered that hotel service in Norseman had little or no finesse. This was the last town before Ceduna, eight hundred miles and ten refreshment stops across the Nullarbor Plain in South Australia, and you could like it or bloody lump it. After a few days of tackling the same no choice dinner menu, I was approached by the formidable Iris, the one and only waitress and built like a Centurion tank.

"Wadyerwant fer yer sweets, Pom?" she barked aggressively.

"I think, Iris, I'll have strawberries and cream by way of a change."

Staring me menacingly in the eye she thundered, "Shit,

Pom, d'yer want port holes in yer bloody coffin?"

There's no convincing answer to that.

"OK, Iris," I acquiesced, "I'll have the usual."

Satisfied that I had resumed an acceptable level of subservience, her hackles retracted as she snarled, "Too bloody right yer will, Pom."

By now I had left my caravan behind at Kalgoorlie. Whether this was a sop for having screwed up my Christmas I do not know but I did not object. I used Norseman as my base for the pre-commissioning of several stations towards the Nullarbor and always kept my room on while overnighting elsewhere.

Returning one Saturday from a week in the sticks, I wandered into the mid-day beer swill at the Railway Hotel. Johnny Nelson, mine host, looked surprised to see me.

"Missed you, Lofty, where have you been?" he asked.

"Out on the route for a week," I replied without thinking.

"Out on the root for a whole bloody week!" cried Johnny as the whole place erupted. "You **must** need a drink, mate!"

Since this seemed to enhance my stock, I made no effort to differentiate between *route* and *root* but I was careful never to use the term again while in Australia.

John's wife, Anne, had quite a different perspective on life. Although she ran a good if robust establishment, her educated Scottish background always seemed better suited to a more cultured setting than Norseman. Anne had her own peculiar sense of humour derived largely from the Australian ballads of Henry Lawson and Banjo Paterson, some of which could be so very easily identified with swinging cosmopolitan Norseman! Among these I recall such masterpieces as *The Digger's London Leave, Holus Bolus, Mad Jack's Cockatoo* and *Clancy of the Overflow*.

Semi-resident Poms were a rare curiosity for the locals in Norseman. The youngsters in particular watched us with close interest. One afternoon I chanced to be at the town's outdoor swimming pool at the same time as a party from the local school. They sat on one side of the pool, we two Poms on the other. At one juncture I dived into the pool and to my horror felt my swimming trunks descend, or rather ascend, to my ankles.

"Cor! The bloody Pom's lost his bathers!" went up the spontaneous roar from a fat, flaxen haired kid as he leapt up and down in triumph.

Quickly retreating to the dressing room lest I should be mistaken for some dastardly pervert, I dried and dressed and beat it back to my hotel.

Later that evening I went with my colleague to the drive-in cinema on the edge of town. The show was split into two halves with an intermission for refreshments. I took my place in the scrimmage at the hot-dog stall and had just reached the counter when, horror of horrors, I stood face to face with the fat, blonde haired kid who was now serving the relishes.

"Hey, it's the bloody Pom what lost his bathers!" he yelled and everyone gawked at me as if I was a freak in a circus show as he gabbled out his story.

One weekend I teamed up with the lads from our Norseman base repair station for a drive down to Esperance on the south coast. At first it was more of the same, gum trees, gum trees and more gum trees. We even went through a town called Salmon Gums.

After that came one of the most beautiful sights imaginable. As we arrived at the edge of the escarpment we looked down on a limitless sea of brilliant orange. It was my first sighting of the Australian Christmas tree and there were millions of them. Not a species you would want in your garden, this member of the mistletoe family is a parasite which surrounds the roots of other trees and plants with a fleshy white ring and them feeds off them. It is a wonderful sight nevertheless.

Standing in Esperance, the view out to sea was more interesting than the town itself. It was fascinating to reflect that, beyond the Archipelago of the Recherché, there was nothing between me and Cape Goodenough in Antarctica and yet here the temperature was closer to boiling point than freezing.

Distance on the Nullarbor is an irrelevance. If you ask how far it is from A to B you invariably get the answer expressed in time and the time depends on your mode of transport. We reckoned on the basis of eighty miles per hour. The postman in Norseman could cover over a hundred miles in the same time, drunk or sober, more often drunk. It usually took him just over an hour to reach Balladonia where there was a fine hotel with a worthy bar. Unfortunately Postie had blotted his copybook at Balladonia and had consequently been banned from the bar. To wreak his revenge, he descended on Balladonia one day complete with electric saw and proceeded to carve up the bar and fell the adjacent telegraph pole before screaming off back to Norseman. Honour restored, normal life resumed.

After Balladonia, the Eyre Highway enters the Nullarbor proper, a vast treeless plain, devoid of any feature or contour, scorched and dry. At that time it had a metal surface as far as the state border at Eucla, then continued as a dust track to Ceduna in South Australia. Driving the ninety-three mile straight towards Caiguna, no bends, no gradients, is a demonic experience if you do it once. Several times a month is the medicine for madness.

Sighting an emu or a kangaroo, or even a discarded Afghan camel is a major event, something of a lottery in fact because all are big and move fast. A 'roo can cross your path at 45 mph, turn on a sixpence and cross you again, if you're lucky. If you hit him, you hope it's on the half-volley, not in full bound as happened in a number of fatalities while I was in that region. A kangaroo through the windscreen at eighty miles an hour is usually terminal.

I always considered it a poor piece of planning that, driving in a westerly direction, the first bend at the end of this straight was followed immediately by a cattle grid. To have sited it shortly before the bend would have been a useful alarm clock to half awake drivers blazing along in auto pilot and always liable to be taken by surprise and overshoot the bend.

It was along this stretch of road that I came across a group of Aborigines, patiently plodding towards their next watering hole. There had been a spate of incidents in which some mindless cretins had shot up the water tanks which had been placed at intervals alongside the road for people in distress and which were much favoured by the Aborigines. Since I was carrying several gallons in jerry cans for my own use, I stopped and offered them a drink. I was intrigued as they each gratefully accepted a very modest amount, no more than essential, then beckoned along the road whence they had come. Sure enough, after a few miles I encountered another group. who behaved as frugally as the first. I found this absolute lack of greed to be extremely impressive. A seasoned old digger had told me back in Coolgardie that the Aborigines in their native environment have one of the, if not the strictest ethical codes on Earth. Violation by an adult can incur very severe retribution. Now I was witnessing their self-discipline for myself.

Generally I was disgusted by the treatment of the blackfellows by the whites. Referred to universally as *boongs*, they were often sneered at and treated as if of lower status than farm animals. Sure enough, the Aborigines hanging about on the fringes of towns were neither one thing nor the other. Having lost their ability to survive in the wild, not qualified to undertake any substantial form of employment, without state support and hooked on cheap wine, they did not make appetising neighbours. The blame for this rests mainly with the immigrants, not the natives. What passes for civilisation for us means destruction for them.

The canniness of the Aborigines was also to be seen along the Eyre Highway. Monster trucks plough their way daily across this main East - West highway. Their drivers need to be tough and invariably are. I recall assisting one grizzly individual in repairing his twenty-second puncture since leaving Sydney. Inevitably some are excessively rough and aggressive and take their pleasures in any way they see fit. To some, the sight of a girl or woman walking unprotected in the middle of nowhere is too much of a temptation, whatever her appearance. So down they come and do their dirty work. Every Aborigine woman knows this so, what do they do for protection? Before the truckie gets to them, they squat at the side of the road and fill their private parts with dust and gravel. This renders them unattractive to even the most depraved truckie. They may take a beating, but they would probably get that anyway. They then clean up at the next water hole.

Our tower erection subcontractors had been briefed about aborigine rights and customs before commencing work on the stations at Yalata and Nunjikompita, both within Aborigine reservations in South Australia. A story came back down the line that one of the things you must not do is to throw a handful of gravel at a native girl as this is a proposal of marriage and failure to honour this pledge can result in death. The erectors were Italians, with their customary eye for the romantic. One of them considered this so fascinating that he tried it. His employers had to get him out of the country within a week.

A feature of the telecommunications system along this sector was to drop and insert wayside channels for provision of telephone links to some of the large isolated ranches. It was at one of these stations, either Crocker or Culver, both named after the local farmers, that one of our engineers heard a knock at the door. Surprised, he opened it to be confronted with an even bigger surprise. There stood the cockie with a coil of wire in his hand. He had apparently been told of his forthcoming telephone service and, the bush telegraph having informed him that an engineer was working at his local station, had come down with the intention of having the wire connected on line. Even more surprising was that he had already connected the other end of the wire to an adjacent fence wire which ran twenty miles back to his homestead! One can appreciate why these guys conquered the continent.

The heat at Caiguna was the fiercest I have ever experienced with a massive forty Fahrenheit degrees diurnal variation. Over 120 degrees in the day, we had to wear woolly sweaters at night when the temperature dropped to 80 degrees. To climb the metal radio tower in the daytime, it was essential to wear gloves. The rexine of the car seats blistered the backs of our thighs. It was like standing in front of an open furnace door. We worked hard and relaxed sensibly there.

One splendid diversion on a Caiguna weekend was a bush drive due south to the sheer cliffs which tower above the Great Australian Bight at this point. There we chanced upon a memorial to John Eyre, the first of the great overlanders, who had arrived here on foot from Fowler Bay in South Australia in 1841. The climate and the terrain thereabouts is indescribably harsh and one wonders how those men held on to their sanity, let alone their lives.

My eye was attracted, at this continental extremity to a piece of shiny, mottled blue rock which differed markedly from the sandy orange conglomerate which stretched to the other three horizons and way beyond. It has taken twenty-eight years for me to discover that it is a piece of banded agate which has reasonable jewellery potential.

No rivers flow into the Great Australian Bight and all the water drawn from the subterranean artesian basin is brackish and undrinkable. At Caiguna there were lines of little glass cloches where the salty water was allowed to evaporate under the glare of the sun before condensing back in a more useable form. Ordinary soap was as useless as a piece of stone in these parts. We did what we could with some special turtle oil concoctions procured back in Norseman.

One of our group had a brainwave at Caiguna. Hearing that it was almost the time for the Melbourne Trots, he made a few enquiries and was informed when the television pictures were to be transmitted over the stand-by radio bearer from Adelaide to Perth. There was no direct monitoring facility at the intermediate points at that time but, by cascading two oscilloscopes, the one triggering the other, it was possible to compile a complete picture, albeit in green and white, on the screen of the second scope. This must be of interest to the people down at the motel, so we duly informed the proprietor and his number two and invited them to come and watch at the appointed hour. They informed all their friends and they informed all their friends. Well, after all, the Trots are the Trots, mate. You can't miss out on an opportunity like that.

We had all the cockies and jackeroos in from miles around. One had driven ninety miles across rough desert to be there. They brought beer and they brought money. Most of them had never seen the Melbourne Trots before although there was no one who hadn't had a punt on them. The beer flowed and the money moved backwards and forwards. Afterwards we retired to the motel and had one of those nights that does not fade from the memory. The stock of the Poms was high.

The love of the Australian for a little wager has never been disputed. Just how far they will go came home to me one day at Caiguna when a puffy little white cloud appeared in the north-eastern sky. Two of the local hands, who had not seen a cloud, never mind rain, for nine months, peered incredulously towards the sky.

"Bet yer she's dropping rain!"

"Five dollars says she's not!"

With that they scrambled into a utility wagon, a *ute* to them, and sped off, bumpety-bump, in a straight line of filthy red dust towards this meteorological freak. When they arrived back, it turned out that they had covered sixty miles chasing the mini cumulus before establishing that it was not depositing any moisture.

No worries, mate, we'll drink to that!

Another day a fellow engineer and I were sipping chilled apricot juice in the local motel when the proprietor, Ernie Fagan, glanced up from counting his takings and asked,

"Say, fellers, isn't this one of your mates coming along the dirt?"

We looked out to see a white Dodge, with give away whip aerial, roaring along ahead of a billowing cloud of thick red dust.

"Who the heck can that be?" we mused.

We were the only team this far east in WA and he was coming from the East.

"Hold on, he's sporting South Australian plates. Christ, it's Gladys!" exclaimed Doug, nearly choking on his juice.

Gladys was the nickname for one of our brightest, most competent and respected engineers. He was extremely fastidious, both about his personal presentation and his job performance. He was also the epitome of an English gentleman, a walking, talking caricature, the ultimate Pommy. Ernie Fagan was the ultimate languid, sand-spitting outback Western Australian.

"God, this should be funny," chortled Doug. "Hey, Ernie, don't let on that we're here."

We withdrew to a recess, out of sight.

In breezed Gladys, head high, eyes bright, instantly taking in all that they surveyed. Ernie carried on counting the contents of his till.

"Thirty-four, thirty-five, thirty-six."

"Ahem."

No reaction.

"Thirty-seven, thirty-eight, thirty-nine."

"Ahem!" slightly louder.

"Yeah?"

"Oh, excuse my interrupting, but does one provide any fare at this time of the arfternoon?"

At which point Ernie dropped all the coins from his hands back into the till while reeling back and exclaiming, "Aw, shit, is this bloke for bloody real?"

Gladys, tilting his head and smiling quizzically, responded, "I'm sorry, old boy, is it something that I said?"

"Jeeesus!" Ernie burst out. "C'mon lads, you take care of him. I can't handle any more of this."

Gladys then turned round to find Doug and me trying to suppress our mirth behind a pillar.

"Welcome to Western Australia," I said.

"Strange place," he muttered. "Are they all like this?"

Ernie had disappeared into the kitchen, his guts aching from laughing.

A few days later I was to have all my faith in Gladys's personal integrity reconfirmed. There was a requirement to take some test equipment to the Mundrabilla site, fifty miles east of Caiguna. On the return journey I was aware that Gladys was working at Eyre, between Caiguna and Mundrabilla. Even though Eyre was several miles off the highway, it seemed polite to call in and pay my respects.

I arrived at the site at one o'clock and there sat Gladys's caravan, gleaming in the sun. Finding the door to the station locked, I walked over to the caravan and, as one would, knocked on the door. Gladys opened the door, greeted me and expressed his surprise at having company so far from anywhere. His surprise was nothing as compared to mine when I saw his table, set out for a solo lunch. Remember, this is three hundred miles from the nearest town, thirty-five miles from the nearest colleagues, ten miles from the nearest road and no visitors expected. There was an immaculate tablecloth, a napkin in its ring, matching cutlery, properly laid for main course and desert, decanter and a wine glass. You have to admire the man. That is what I call gentility.

One of the other ultra-English gentlemen on our force

was Jeremy, also bright and extremely competent but viewed antipathetically by your average Australian. We had two heavy duty truck drivers who hauled all the equipment, mail and victuals up from Fremantle on a once weekly schedule, picking up any empty crates on the return journey. Terry hailed from Subiaco, Sooby City as he proudly called it. He was always beaming whatever the conditions, always confidentially dropping the word from the streets on which nickel mine was next to do a Poseidon.

"Hill 23, Lofty, keep it under your hat."

What he thought I could do with such treasured information stuck at the wrong end of a five hundred mile single wire with earth return telephone line, I do not know. But he was a real gem, a great guy to know.

His fellow driver was a Tasmanian, former Victoria clay-pigeon shooting champion and previously employed on the oil rigs in the Bass Strait. A nice guy if you didn't rub him up the wrong way, but quite different in character and disposition to Terry. Unfortunately Jeremy always got under Rick's skin.

"You're behind schedule, Harris," he sternly stated.

It was well known to the rest of us that, as he collected the empty equipment crates from each station, Rick would join up with the local cockies for a spot of 'roo shooting. He would dump the skins and tails in his truck, sell them off in Fremantle and shell out the proceeds on his return.

"Yer little Pommy bastard!" he snarled, picking the diminutive Jeremy off the ground and hurling him, as if in a dwarf tossing contest, on to the top of his loaded trailer.

"Get down from there if you bloody can," he growled.

"I'm sorry, Harris, this will be the subject of a memo to headquarters."

Rick grimaced testily up into the sun-filled sky.

"Quit while yer've got the chance, yer stupid Pommy bastard."

Nothing more was said. There was to be no memorandum.

I had always admired the bravery and skill of the Australian flying doctor service and had often seen it in operation on film. It gave me considerable satisfaction therefore to be invited to assist one evening at Caiguna. There had been a nasty road accident a little way east of Caiguna involving a couple on honeymoon, and one of the victims required urgent hospitalisation. We were told that the flying doctor was already on his way from Kalgoorlie, but that it would be dark by the time he arrived. Everyone with a vehicle to hand was asked to flank the simple grass landing strip behind the motel with headlamps to be switched on at a given signal.

After a while we lit up and shortly thereafter in he came on a perfect landing. It was all hands to the plough as we helped with carrying the injured, marshalling the plane and carrying out the doctor's bidding. In what seemed next to no time we were back in our vehicles with lights on as the doughty little aircraft bumped its way down the grass track and disappeared into the night. Well earned drinks all round and much bewilderment as to what there is to do on honeymoon on the Nullarbor.

You really do feel remote between Caiguna and Eucla on

the state border. The in-between stations were Eyre, Mundrabilla, Madura, and Hampton in that order. There are two places to get a drink on this one hundred and twenty-five mile stretch, Cocklebiddy, forty miles beyond Caiguna, and Madura, a further thirty-five miles on. My first stop at Cocklebiddy was my last. Expansion of their customer base was decidedly not one of their top priorities.

Between Eyre and Mundrabilla there is some topographical respite from the universal flatness. There, the escarpment which to the west has formed the edge of the Great Australian Bight, comes inland. Taking advantage of this variation in height for radio propagation line-of-sight purposes, Mundrabilla had been sited on the top of the scarp. providing an approach track of some interest.

I was alone up there one evening, relaxing after work by indulging in a little practice on a dart board which I had inherited with the caravan on site. Unbeknown to me, I was being watched by three Aborigines. What they made of this strange performance only they know. Revealing themselves when they felt inclined to do so, they continued to watch in amusement until I invited one of them to try for himself. Clutching the arrow like a javelin, he hurled it at the board from nine feet and missed by twenty. Patiently I coaxed his gnarled fingers into a more delicate grip and demonstrated the preferred method of projection. Scoring did not matter, the bull's eye was all. They took it in turns for long enough, brows furrowed in concentration until the great moment of rejoicing when one of them hit the inner. You could not get more excitement if England won the Ashes. Such was their enthusiasm that I gave them the board and the darts. and off they toddled into the bush, jabbering excitedly and waving as they went.

A strange experience befell me between Madura and Eucla on a day on which I was recovering some test equipment from Eucla. First of all my radiator dried up and I was short of water. After letting it cool for some time I poured in what water I had and supplemented by having a pee in it, a ploy I had learned from the APO boys in Norseman. Gingerly I proceeded on to Eucla where I knew that I would be able to take on extra water. I made it and loaded the equipment and water onto my vehicle . I then decided to have a cigarette.

"Hey, hang on, where's my lighter?"

I was really proud of that lighter. A silver Ronson, inscribed with my initials, it had been given to me by my father on my twenty-first birthday while I was serving with the Royal Signals in Germany. I turned out my pockets, I turned out the cab of the truck, I searched the station floor and the compound. Nothing. I was gutted. Dad had just died and that lighter was a constant reminder of him. As I sombrely trundled westward out of Eucla I tried to think back to when I had smoked my last cigarette. Yes, that was it, when the radiator boiled up. But where the hell was that? Somewhere between Madura and Eucla to be sure, but that's fifty miles on a road that is as straight and featureless as the tracks of the Trans-Siberian Railway. Then, inspiration, divine intervention. I recalled a mental image of our radio tower at Hampton, west-south-west of where I was parked; I was sure I had seen it, a couple of miles across the plain.

I chuckled to myself as I thought of Hampton. The site surveyors had selected this spot in the middle of nowhere, no geographical or aboriginal name to help them. Just a blank patch in the desert surrounded by shimmering heat, giving the feeling of being alone on an island. There was to sit a two hundred feet high tower, rising out of the plain like an erect phallus. Yes, that's it, a Hampton, and so it was named.

As I approached the possible area, my hopes began to slump. The Eyre Highway is bordered by millions of discarded drinks cans at all stages of decay. I was driving directly into an enormous setting sun. Looking for anything there would be like looking for a needle in a haystack. As soon as Hampton tower came into view I slowed right down and crept along.

"No joy," I thought, "this trip will take for ever."

As I pressed my foot on the accelerator yet another can glinted in the reflected rays of the occidental sun.

"That was a bit bright," thought I.

Screeching to a stop, I leapt down from my cab and ran back to where I thought the glint had come from. There in the middle of that wilderness was my precious lighter.

Breaking the hot, dusty drive across the Nullarbor, I wandered thirstily into the motel bar at Madura. As soon as I entered the place I knew I had done the wrong thing. It was pay day and all the jackeroos for miles around had come in to drink their earnings. Some already had and lay slumped across the tables. Others were involved in a game of darts that looked and sounded more like Amazonian warfare. The furniture was crude and bore many battle scars.

One could excuse those fence riders for having the occasional blow-out. The sheep stations which they patrolled measured their perimeter fences not in miles but in hundreds of miles. Mundrabilla was one of the biggest. In unrelenting temperatures of a hundred and above the brain and body are under severe threat unless they have some suitable safety valve.

Dressed as I was in the local style, bush hat, tatty shorts, thongs and brown as a berry to boot, I picked my way across to the bar under the illusion that no one would suspect my origins.

Wrong!!!

"Say, mate, you a Pom?"

How the hell did he know?

"Yes, as a matter of fact I am. What are you drinking?"

"I'll drink yer bloody beer, Pom."

Slurp, it had gone.

"Pommy bastard!"

"Fill him up again, mate," I whispered to the barman.

"Not a bad bastard for a Pom. I'll drink yer bloody beer."

My new mucker swilled his way through half a dozen jars before I had finished my second.

"Say, Pom, comin' outside ter splash yer boots?".

The invitation was irresistible, but I resisted.

"No mate, you go, I've just had one," I lied, crossing my legs in desperation.

The barman crept closer.

"Hey, Pom, did old Harry ask you outside?"

"Er, yes, in a manner of speaking he did," I replied.

"Shit, mate, he likes you. Old Harry only fights with his friends."

It is politick at watering holes in the Australian bush to pay for your drinks as you order them. This facilitates a quick escape when required. I had no hesitation on this occasion in accepting the barman's kind advice and beating the hell out of Madura like a ferret up a drainpipe.

Eucla was to be our last station. A separate team was making its way from the Adelaide end and we would connect up at Eucla. I arrived to take up residence at the Eucla motel with Jonathan, a Cambridge graduate with all the hallmarks of a whiz-kid. We checked in and drove round to our rooms where we found two chalet maids preparing them for the new occupants.

"Halloo!" shouted one.

"Good God, Oxford!" snorted Jonathan, without hesitation.

"Cambridge!" she responded with the utmost languor.

I had always sensed that I was at a disadvantage in the world of academia, now I knew it.

Eucla was a pleasant station for the short time we were there. We had a little skippy for company at breakfast each morning and pressure seemed a million miles away. The station itself was an education. Built as a back to back radio terminal, it had a makeshift packing case screen down the middle to separate the South Australians from the Western Australians. Just as well for ne'er the twain shall meet.

The WA guys generally dressed for comfort, scruffy T-shirt, baggy shorts and flip-flops. Their SA counterparts could not have presented a bigger contrast, white shirts, immaculately pressed with box pleats, white shorts with razor sharp creases, long white socks to the knee and stylish shoes. The attitudes matched. We had come to like the WA boys and had taken on some of their easy attitude as a defence against the harsh environment It came as a rude shock to meet the starchy stand-offishness from the other side. But they were very businesslike and efficient and that was what the job required if it was going to be a success.

One of our lads from the SA side told me of a trip he had made along the Birdsville trail from Port Pirie to the Queensland border. Arriving at Birdsville, which is just about as remote as you can go, his eyes fell on the local hotel, not much of a place to be sure but, after what he had endured, it had the look of Paradise. He went in, hot, parched and famished and sat at a table. Two disenchanted looking biddies were eyeing him up from across the room, squatting indecorously on their back to front chairs.

"Do you have any tucker?" he asked.

"Yeah, wait there," cackled one as she dragged herself towards the kitchen.

The other slouched after her seconds later. After enough time to prepare a seven course dinner, the elder of the two stomped in and deposited a plate of cold mutton in front of him. Nothing else, just cold, fatty mutton.

"Er, don't you have any vegetables?"

"Yer don't get no rain in Birdsville; yer don't get no bloody vegetables in Birdsville."

"OK then, do you have any sauces?"

"Hey, Mary, fetch the ketchup, there's a bloody Pommy out here what thinks it's Christmas."

He ate what he could, left and drove on, wondering whether there was a Heaven beyond Hell.

After the months of installation and testing it was now time to connect the system through at Eucla, giving a continuous radio path from Adelaide through to Perth. At this point it is worth introducing another of our commissioning engineers, a Canadian named Burt who had worked with us across Western Australia.

Burt was no ordinary mortal. In his earlier career he had been working on an Early Warning System up in Alaska in the depths of winter when he received an urgent call to drop everything and get himself down to Jamaica. He was the first and probably the last passenger to arrive at Kingston Airport clad in a parka and snowboots. Not that this would phase him one jot. Brilliant at his job and experienced in some of the harshest working environments on Earth, Burt had a self-confidence and a pleasant belligerence that endeared him to his colleagues and at the same time put the fear of God into them.

Until now, the only means of communication between radio sites had been either over single sideband radio or, wherever possible, over the Engineer's Order Wire utilising that part of the system that had so far been installed. Discipline on the Order Wire was pretty good. Conversation was businesslike and crisp, generally because one did not know who might be listening in at an intermediate or remote station. Such niceties never bothered Burt. Many an ear had been singed by the streams of invective delivered in a highly charged Canadian *fortissimo*. Indeed, the announcement in any station that Burt was on the Order Wire was reason enough to break off from a meal, or whatever one happened to be doing, to rush into the radio room for some high class entertainment.

Burt had a strange affinity for equine faeces. Every conversation contained at least three horse shits. This had been evident since Day One. But on this day when we were celebrating the through connection of the system, someone had forgotten to tell Burt. Access to the Order Wire at each station was via microphone and ear-phones, with the notable exception of the terminals at Perth and Adelaide. These were fully working Australian Post Office stations with other existing systems and with a very strict procedural discipline in force. Moreover the incoming Order Wire transactions came in, not through headphones, but through high volume loudspeakers.

Burt was still carrying out some tests back on the Norseman - Caiguna section, blissfully unaware of his new audience. Having requested a spot frequency from Norseman he was not amused by what he received.

"What mother fucker sent me that fucking horse shit?" boomed out simultaneously in Adelaide and Perth.

Let us just say that the powers-that-be in both state capitals were not amused and formal apologies became necessary.

At long last I set off with Doug on the long road back to Perth and ultimately Blighty. It was difficult to take in how much ground we had covered and after a full Sunday's driving we checked in at the Palace Hotel in Kalgoorlie. It all seemed so much quieter and peaceful than when we had last been there, more like Aberdeen on a flag day. Hannan Street was virtually deserted as we wandered along looking in the shop windows. Up the hill on the left-hand side we came across a music shop and there inside was a piano. I have always enjoyed tickling the ivories although my repertoire is not very extensive without sheet music. Moreover I had not played for the best part of a year. Still, I could not resist it.

The shop was empty as I sat down and rent the air with an enthusiastic rendering of Chopin's *Polonaise in A Major*. Doug looked on in amazement. No, the old touch hadn't completely deserted me. I rattled on playing the complete work before throwing my hands in the air with a final magnificent flourish.

I turned round to see a little old lady with grey hair, pince-nez spectacles, and tears flowing down her cheeks.

"Oh!" she said in a soft English accent, "I haven't heard music played like that since I left the Old Country."

Having ascertained that we were from the Old Country, she added, "They are all Philistines around here you know." That was the pinnacle of my musical career.

The dear old soul was almost as sad a case as the two ex-Mansfield miners I met in the bar of the Palace Hotel. On seeing my open return ticket from Perth to Heathrow they both burst into tears. Having emigrated on Ten Pound passages, neither had been able to save enough for a one-way ticket home. The more they hated Australia, the more they drank and the more they drank, the less chance they had of leaving Australia, a vicious circle with no hope of escape.

I met up with Big Jim again on the final leg back to Perth. We stopped at No. 7 Tank to recover a dipole from the radio tower. I climbed up and was lowering the contrivance down to Jim when I spotted a huge brown snake heading through the bush in a direct line towards him.

"Snake!" I yelled from two hundred feet up.

I faintly caught, "What, Blue?"

I wriggled my right arm in what I hoped was a snake like manner.

"Snake!!" I bawled, even louder.

"Sorry, Blue, I can't hear you," came back his dulcet Liverpudlian tones.

Just then he spotted the enemy for himself and darted away to safety. I realised that my voice had been carried away on the wind which was quite fresh at the top of the tower. We completed the task and I descended to *terra firma*.

I was immediately confronted by Big Jim who asked seriously, "Did you see that bloody big snake, Blue?"

Time to go home, I thought, and we drove leisurely down to the big city.

Perth was the perfect place to rehabilitate back into the human race after the deprivations of the Nullarbor. Wearing a collar and tie to dinner took a bit of getting used to but the quality of the food and wine in its many delightful restaurants was ample compensation. Varied menus, no portholes in one's coffin, a wide choice of vegetables and polite, efficient service had become distant memories.

I enjoyed exploring the parks, with their enormous Karri trees, and the relaxing walks by the Swan River. A drive down to Bunbury, taking in the quaint little church at Australind, the smallest in Australia, gave me an appreciation of the fertile Garden of the West, with its vineyards, forests of giant trees, orchards and farms.

Scarborough Beach was another place not to be missed, but here again a myth was exploded. Whoever said that Australians love the great outdoors? It was always either too hot or too cold for our hosts. They much preferred to be under shelter, nursing a frostie.

Lovely though it was, Perth was frustrating. I was always itching to do my final packing and board the plane that would take me back to the family I had missed so much for so long.

The route home, again on a BOAC 707 is worth recording, not a route one could take nowadays: Perth - Singapore - New Delhi - Teheran - Tel-Aviv - Frankfurt - Heathrow. As we passed over the Bay of Bengal, one of the starboard engines gave up the ghost and we limped into New Delhi where we were to be grounded for ten hours. It was most disconcerting to see an Indian aircraft maintenance technician peering under the arc lights at a diagram of a Boeing engine part and trying uncertainly to match it up to the jet engine above his head. We were told that there was a complete spare engine at Karachi airport but that the state of politics between India and Pakistan at that time rendered that inaccessible. Great was my joy therefore when I heard that another spare had been located in Teheran and was on its way. We made it, late but relieved.

See yer, sport.

Chapter 3
The White Man's Grave

Sitting behind a desk in a crowded planning office in England was something of a change from the solitude and deprivations of the Nullarbor. The important thing was that I was back with my family. But once you have been labelled *An Overseas Man* by British industry, it is difficult to throw it off.

I continued to work in the export field, applying myself to further extensions in Australia and the planning of the Santiago - Arica radio transmission system in Chile until the Allende affair put a stop to that. I was itching to get involved in a Bolivia project which was then under way, urged on by my frustrated mountaineering instincts. This was not to be. Like so many of my colleagues I was committed to planning the overlay of the Nigerian national telephone network.

It was a quiet Friday afternoon in May 1972 when the Overseas Contracts Manager came up to my desk from behind, laid a hand on my shoulder and said, "Can I have a word with you, young man?"

The new Project Co-ordinator for Nigeria had been selected, invited and, after family consultation, had accepted. The fundamental difference between this assignment and Australia was that I would now be accompanied by my wife and two young daughters. Whether this was fair to my family was a question I wrestled with night after night. The Biafran war had only recently ended and some of the stories reaching us from

Lagos were more suited to the horror fiction shelves of the local library.

"Don't worry," I was reassured, "it will develop your character."

During that weekend, unbeknown to me at the time, my departmental manager had flown to Lagos on business. As he arrived, in the early morning, the roads were just beginning to become congested. By the time he reached Carter Bridge, linking the mainland with Lagos Island, the go-slow had started in earnest. Off came his jacket, followed by his tie. Up went the shirt sleeves, down went the window.

"Churriiist!!! What in God's name is that?"

He had never visited Lagos before and was now encountering the fragrance of the city's night-soil for the first time as it made its way across the bridge in a convoy of trucks to be deposited in the lagoon.

"It is de shit, Sir," he was politely informed by the driver.

Considering his options as he sat static in the traffic, and seeing no way that his situation was likely to improve by venturing further into this hell hole, he returned immediately to the airport and boarded the first flight home. By the time he recited his tale of woe, I had already signed up for two eighteen month tours of duty.

When we took up residence, there were twenty-six thousand expatriates living in and around Lagos, each one of whom had his or her own bemusing stories to tell. Some were clearly exaggerated, most were based on actual occurrences, some were absolutely hilarious. Needless to say my own compendium of bizarre experiences grew from day one.

Our project office was a rented first floor property in a colourful cul-de-sac on Lagos Island. Everything went on in that street, vending, cooking, puncture repair, welding, signwriting, poultry rearing, gambling, to name but a few. There was a constant cacophony of shouting, car horns, cock crowing, goat bleating and piledrivers. It was never dull.

My arrival in the company office was greeted by an enthusiastic array of beaming black faces. I certainly felt very welcome. The UK based staff were all familiar to me from the introductory parties which we had attended earlier.

My first requirement on settling in was for a pee. I was kindly pointed in the right direction, through a door at the far end of the office. When I opened it I nearly fainted. The stench was unbelievable. Holding my breath and peering in I observed a Shanks & McEwan full of everything bar water. It looked as though the whole of Lagos had had diarrhoea in there since it had last been flushed. I'd seen some disgusting dunnies in Australia (oh, the heat and the flies!) but this was unrivalled.

I staggered back into the main office and grabbed the fellow closest to me.

"What is that?" I demanded, pointing towards the firmly closed door.

"It is a door, Sir," he replied, wondering which planet this new *oga* had just arrived from.

"Beyond the door," I explained. "That toilet is foul and you sit here next to it all day and every day."

71

"Ah, Sir, we are having no water since three weeks."

"Three weeks!" I gasped, "It looks more like three years."

"Yes, Sir."

"What is your name again?"

"Mr. Aromere, Sir."

Very appropriate, thought I.

"Right, Mr. Aromere, do you know what is disinfectant?"

Blank look followed by "No, Sir."

Earlier I had spotted a very bright looking accounts clerk.

"Joseph, are you familiar with disinfectant?"

"Yes, Sir, San Izal, Sir, Pine, Sir."

Clearly my initial assessment had been accurate.

"Well done, Joseph. Take our friend here to the local supermarket and purchase a bottle of disinfectant."

They returned from Maloney's half an hour later with San Izal and receipt. I took the bottle, ventured into the toilet and quickly dispensed the whole contents into the Stygian mire. Immediately there was a change of aroma. I turned to Mr. Aromere, whose face was contorted in disgust.

"There, Mr. Aromere, is that not an improvement?" I asked confidently.

"No, Sir, I prefer de smell of de shit."

After ten days, I, like all others before me, succumbed, to the revenge of Montezuma.

"You did well," our Irish finance manager informed me. "Most people go under in less than a week."

The next few days were hell, dashing from throne to throne, always terrified that the unrelenting Lagos traffic would frustrate me. The last straw was a banner which appeared above my desk reading:

"HAPPINESS IS A DRY FART".

The gentleman from whom I took over, a dry humoured fellow from Sunderland, was observing my baptism with quiet amusement. He'd been there, done it, seen the lot and, in all circumstances, knew what to expect. I learned a lot from Greg.

One morning during that first week, Greg picked me up from our apartment - there was no way I dared to drive in that traffic yet - and proceeded out of our road onto the main Awolowa Road.

Peeeep!

A shrill whistle blasted and a purposeful looking traffic policeman strode up to Greg's open window.

"Ah, de European causing confusion, eh?"

"Sorry, Sergeant, I misread your signal, Sergeant."

"You disobey de Road Traffic Decree Section. I am not de sergeant, I am de corporal!"

"Oh, I'm sorry, Corporal, you have the demeanour of a sergeant."

"Oh, thank you, Sir, you may proceed, Sir."

With less *savoir faire* that little confrontation could have cost plenty dash.

The Dutch have been trying to cultivate a black tulip for centuries; we had a black Hyacinth in our office. Hyacinth was the messenger and covered vast tracts of the city each day on foot. It was usually faster than using the driver as the traffic hardly moved. The trouble with Hyacinth was that he took everything one said to him literally.

We had a constant stream of totally unsuitable job seekers, donation seekers, vendors and other undesirables making the trek up to the first floor and marching into the office unchallenged. Hyacinth was appointed doorman, in addition to his other duties. His instructions were to let no one into the office who did not have official business with us.

One morning there was a terrible row going on at the door. I went out to investigate and there were about twenty people, mostly Nigerian but including two of our European subcontractors, all trying to push their way in while being efficiently repelled by Hyacinth and Tayo, the office driver.

"What the hell is going on?" I asked.

"Sir," proclaimed Hyacinth, "Sir, I not let in anyone until I check de papers. I only read slow, sir, and de others must wait."

It often worked out like that, solve one problem and create a much bigger problem.

Opposite the office, construction had started on a multi-storey office block. Every day from 8 a.m. until 5 p.m. we heard and felt the constant thump, thump, thump of a pile-driver. It registered two ounces on the office postage scales. From that and from timing the periodicity at four seconds I calculated that the force hitting my brain was equivalent to 7.232 tons per day or thirty six tons a week. Contract work in Nigeria can cause headaches but this was way into the insanity zone.

One of our finance staff, fresh in from England was bemused by the goings on across the road and spent hours each day giving a running commentary on what was happening. A huge trailer bowled up one morning with thirty tons of cement in one hundredweight bags. Two labourers in loin cloths formed a human chain transferring it to the site. As they passed the truck, a bag was deposited on their heads, from where they wheeled away at a trot into the compound, depositing the bags, without stopping, onto an ever increasing pile. As the day went on their bodies gradually changed from ebony black to Persil white.

After a long break, our commentator muttered in a deadpan Geordie accent, "Away man, all they need is a shower of rain and they'll set solid."

Another Geordie, or to be more accurate, a Wearside accent emanated from a most unlikely source on the day in 1973 on which Leeds United met Sunderland in the FA Cup final at Wembley. Leeds, at that time boasting such luminaries as Bremner, Hunter, Lorimer and Giles, were odds-on favourites to beat a modest Sunderland outfit languishing in the Second Division of the Football League.

The usual crop of expatriate families were lazing around the Ikoyi Club pool, as was their wont on Saturday afternoons. Parading along the side of the pool was the Jayne Mansfield of West Africa, the very well structured April of Leventis. All the husbands had seen this remote blonde goddess whenever they had picked up their wives at the Leventis hairdressing salon on Marina. Most imagined her to be exotic Mediterranean dream material.

The playful banter of the frolicking kids was suddenly interrupted by an excited voice announcing that Sunderland had beaten Leeds 1-0. This was followed immediately by a huge splash as April fell backwards, fully dressed into the water.

"Quick," shouted one eager would be lifeguard, "April of Leventis has fallen in!"

"Bugger April of Leventis," came the gurgle from the pool, "I'm Gladys of bloody Sunderland."

How illusions are shattered!

After a hard day at work, the Ikoyi Club was the ideal retreat for refreshment and recuperation. There were certain time honoured rules there in addition to the published rules. The first three seats at the bar were reserved for employees of the United Africa Company and were seldom unoccupied. One evening after work, one of the UAC lads rolled in, creased in laughter. There was a reverent silence awaiting his tale.

Apparently he was approaching the T-junction at Moloney's supermarket when he spotted a traffic policeman in the middle of the junction. The officer, with eye-balls rolling, had both arms in the air, flipping his hands away from his body in a repeat clenching movement, while rotating continually in a clock-wise direction. Our UAC friend watched this for several minutes with intrigue, then, glancing right and left and in his rear-view mirror, realised that his was the only vehicle in sight. So he edged nervously into a left turn, but, as he passed the policeman, a huge hand banged down on the roof of his car.

As he stopped a head appeared at his open window

demanding, "What colour am I?"

Now that is a sensitive question in Nigeria and our UAC man was no fool.

"You are brown, Officer."

"No I am not brown. What colour am I?"

Taking his life into his hands, UAC ventured, "You're black, Officer."

"No I am not black!" fizzed back the policeman and flipping his fingers alternately in inward and outward motions he screamed, "When I do dis I am green and when I do dat I am red."

In actual fact colour of skin was never a problem. Nigerians liked to call us *oyingbo* (white) and we duly responded with *dudu* (black) with no hard feelings on either side. When one of our British engineers brought his Ibo fiancee to a party to announce their engagement she appeared in a skimpy black mini-dress and bright orange wig.

"Good God, Paula," gasped one of the guests, "all you need are white stripes and you can stand in for a Belisha beacon!"

This would cause great offence in the politically correct circles of today. At that time it was funny to Nigerians and Europeans alike.

It did not take long to deduce that the enmity between tribes was greater than any disapproval on their part of Europeans. Tribalism had instigated the Biafra War and it was going to take more than political compromises to heal the wounds.

One evening my Ibo steward, Tony, called me to his

quarters where his infant daughter was in a high fever and foaming at the mouth. I immediately took father and daughter to our Company doctor, a Greek paediatrician. He did what he could and wrote out a referral to the Lagos City Hospital.

It was very late in the evening when we arrived at the hospital registration office. Several people were wandering around, some sleeping in the waiting area, but there was nobody waiting at the office window. Tony stood there appealing in vain for someone to attend to his daughter. After several minutes had passed, I went to the window myself and noticed a Yoruba girl dozing over a desk in an adjoining room. Calling her in my most authoritative voice, I eventually attracted her reluctant attention. Tony cited his problem.

She looked at him for several seconds before asking disparagingly, "What tribe are you?"

She knew damned well what tribe he was. I nearly exploded.

"It does not matter in the slightest what tribe he is, his daughter is critically ill."

She glanced disinterestedly at the baby girl who was still convulsing, and signed off with, "There is no doctor on duty until morning. You will wait"

She then returned to her desk and lowered her head onto her arm.

There was no way I could enter the registration office and little to be achieved if I could, so I told Tony to remain seated and strode off along a corridor until I found a genuine looking doctor. Having listened to my complaint, he summoned a colleague, briefed him and assured me that all would be taken care of. And it was. The little girl was treated while Tony and I combined in the completion of a registration form. When it became apparent that I, not Tony, would be settling the bill, the attitude of the registration clerk changed. By that time, however, she had lost all my respect.

The local press was a source of constant amusement. One could chuckle at and excuse the occasional typographical error such as,

"Fire in Apongbon Street: Much valuable
equipment, including trypewriters, destroyed."

Such slips occur in all papers across the globe. Some of the articles however were a hoot. Take this one.

Three days before Nigeria switched from driving on the left hand side of the road to driving on the right, a notice appeared in the national press advising everyone that government and military vehicles must change over on the Monday and all private and commercial vehicles on the Tuesday. It's true, absolutely true!

On the morning after Concorde set the speed record for a flight from Johannesburg to London a headline appeared in the national press informing readers that a mystery enemy had declared war on Nigeria and had dropped bombs on Maiduguri. It transpired that the sound barrier had been broken overhead.

On more than one occasion, a wanted notice would appear in the press seeking

"Man, dark complexion, black curly hair, wide nostrils,
thick lips, brown eyes."

Never saw him, guv!
A bold headline hailed,

"Nigerian Navy conquers Atlantic"

Apparently a frigate had successfully concluded a courtesy visit to New York.

I always feel some sympathy for the navies of developing countries as they usually come a poor third in the queue for finance. Nigeria was no exception in the seventies. A huge army was a necessity, not so much to defend the borders as to quell the frequent insurrection from within. Three British frigates called in at Lagos during our time there, including *HMS Salisbury* on its way to man the Beira blockade off Mozambique. During one visit refuelling manoeuvres were undertaken with the Nigerian Navy. One British officer revealed afterwards that he would sooner carry out such an exercise with a NATO ship in a force ten Arctic gale than with a Nigerian vessel on an equatorial mill pond.

One such courtesy call coincided with a visit by the high riding footballers of Manchester City, at that time a powerful force in the English game. The resident Brits were highly excited at the thought of what they would do to the local teams. Indeed, when they took on Jos Mighty Jets they were brilliant for the first five minutes and quickly went a goal up. Then the heat and humidity got to them and Jos ran out easy winners by four goals to one. When they appeared together with two ships' companies of the Royal Navy at the Ikoyi Club, there was great anticipation of some serious frustration letting.

In the event, there was no trouble. A well schooled boatswain had warned the members that an earlier than usual departure would be prudent; big Joe Corrigan and his Manchester team mates were decorum itself. The only hint of possible trouble to come was early in the evening when the first matelot, a huge barrel chested Tyneside stoker in naval uniform, approached the bar and requested three bottles of Star beer.

"I cannot serve you, Sir, you are not wearing a tie," trotted out the pint sized barman with practised nonchalance.

He suddenly found himself a foot and a half further off the ground and held tightly at the neck.

"Three pints of bloody Star!"

This time there was plenty of chalance.

"Yessir, coming Sir, three bottles Sir!"

Service after that was excellent.

There was much *bonhomie* but no subsequent trouble in the club. We heard next day that the usual inter-ship melee had taken place back at the quay on Marina, but thankfully an international incident had been avoided and all club staff and members were intact.

The Nigerian Green Eagles were at that time a respected force in African football but no more than that. There was a fierce traditional rivalry with Ghana and with Kenya, but no hint of their imminent emergence as a force to be reckoned with on the world stage. Their athletes too have thrived on international competition and this from a very humble base in the Seventies.

It was disrespectfully reported that Nigeria had won three

gold medals at the previous Olympic Games, heading the shot, catching the javelin and the hundred Naira dash.

It was also reported that an optimistic Irishman had appeared at the competitors' entrance with a roll of wire mesh under his arm and announced himself as "Murphy, Ireland, fencing."

Not everything was to be believed.

Not all the laughs were on the Nigerians. They found us very comical as we tried to come to terms with their customs and culture and I'm sure there are many hilarious stories circulating in the Nigerian community about the stupid antics of the expats. One chap, an Austrian freight-forwarder, used to walk around Lagos, much to the amusement of the locals, in *lederhosen* and feathered cap. Some years later when I enquired after his health, I was told that he was now traipsing around Vienna in Nigerian agbada, not quite so amusing to the stodgy Viennese.

Irish friends of ours had a huge floppy pawed hound which they optimistically deployed as a guard dog. A hand full of peanuts and he was anybody's. They had acquired him from an expat. in Ibadan and were driving home with the beast for the first time when they ran into a traffic snarl up stretching for several miles coming into Lagos. Spotting his opportunity the dog was out of the window and off at an easy canter along the Ikorodu Road.

This happened at a time when all was not well on the Indian sub-continent, especially in the Dacca area, and the mayhem was being reported daily through the world's news outlets The previous owners of our four legged friend had unfortunately named him Bangladesh.

It was a very self-conscious Irishman therefore who was seen galloping along the crowded Ikorodu Road shouting, "Bangladesh, Bangladesh, Bangladesh!"

He fully expected to be either arrested as a political activist or locked up as a nut case. He wasn't and he recovered his pooch, glad to say, which he promptly renamed Paddy-Paws.

There was another incident involving a dog, a mangy, sorry looking specimen that parked itself at the door of our apartment. Nothing would persuade it to leave and it became a real problem. Not knowing whether it was rabid or not, we could not keep stepping over it and the kids were too small to let near it. Someone suggested putting down cayenne pepper, which we did. The mutt just lapped it up and looked for more. Every time the gardener took it out of the compound it just returned.

Eventually I had to go to the local police station to seek the address of the stray animal unit, if there was such a thing.

"No," I was told "the constable will accompany you and investigate the case of the mad dog."

The compound was separated from the road by a ranch fence at each end of which were vehicle access gates. The constable investigated, concluded that the dog was mad and something should be done about it. I had already got that far myself. We left him to it and retired indoors while he prowled around outside.

After half an hour he knocked at the door and, standing there with a Watsonian smirk on his face, confided, "I have solved de case of de mad dog, Sir. De problem was dat you did not shut de gates."

Looking at him in disbelief, I started, "But we've got a ranch fence."

Oh, save your breath, I thought.

I finished up by wrapping the dog in an old sheet, driving it to the remotest part of the island and turning it loose, whereon it struck up an immediate alliance with a pig which was scavenging around. Problem not solved but passed on.

The golf caddies at the Ikoyi Club had a lot of fun with the expat golfers. Many of these kids were no mean golfers themselves but were required to be totally subservient to the players for whom they caddied. They trundled around the course in their bare feet, hunting out wayward balls from the most inhospitable undergrowth. They had perfected the art of lifting the ball with their toes and walking without any visible change of stride before depositing it in a more, or less, favourable lie, depending upon which player they had placed their bet to win. Many, many expat golfers were totally confused by the position in which their ball had come to lie, not least the professionals competing in the Nigerian Open. To verbally abuse your caddie was a sure way to finish up behind a tree with no direct line to fairway or putting surface. They were good lads, most of the time, and well remunerated. As with the pickers (ball boys) on the adjacent tennis courts, life would have been a good deal more difficult without them.

Another group with whom the expatriates had a love-hate relationship were the car minders. Wherever one parked there was an immediate phalanx of minders vying for business. Hiring them guaranteed nothing but shooing them off was an open invitation to interfere with the vehicle as soon as it was left unattended. This happened not only in the city but also on the coastal road by the beaches.

We were particularly fond of Victoria beach as a Sunday venue but the parking always irritated me, until that is I found Liverpool. I've never been a Liverpool supporter, always reserving my favours for Nottingham Forest but I became very fond of the red-shirted warrior who frequented Victoria Beach.

Our acquaintance began one Sunday morning when parking slots were at a premium. The minders were jostling each other and my family, all trying to grab a beach bag or a deck chair, and things were looking quite nasty when, across the road, I spotted this huge fellow, I would say about seventeen years old, with muscles like Popeye and wearing a red shirt with LIVERPOOL emblazoned across back and front. Clearing my throat I uttered a bellow that would have enchanted the Kop.

"**LIVERPOOL!**" I roared.

The jostling stopped, the crowd fell back and up strode the Nigerian equivalent of a Scouser.

"Yes, Sir?"

"You are my man, Liverpool, today and every Sunday. I pay you top rate."

"Yes, Sir, I am your man. Shoo!"

With that all the minor urchins departed and left me, my family and my car in peace and safety thereafter.

I had a lot of respect for our Nigerian counterparts. We

often lost sight of the fact that we had grown up in a high tech environment, always living and working on the leading edge of technological development. Some of those lads were confronting the technology for the first time in their lives and how fast they absorbed it! As one senior Ministry official told me, his grandfather had never seen an aeroplane and his father never saw television and here was I expecting him to be able to determine the relative qualities of two microchips, the circuitry of which he had never previously encountered. They negotiated a very steep learning curve with considerable skill and endeavour.

Occasionally the technology would get the better of them, as on the day I was called to the office of the Chief Maintenance Engineer.

"We have a problem, short of some spare parts," he winced.

"Tell me which and I will see what we can do," I offered.

"We have no *disting*" he said.

"No what?" I asked.

"No *disting*. Have you any of er, *disting* at your Oshodi stores?"

"Do you have a part number for the *disting*?" I asked hopefully.

"No, er, I am thinking how to describe it, you know, er, *disting*."

"I am very sorry but I do not know. On what part of the system is the *disting* used?"

"On the regulator by-pass."

We were making progress.

"Do you mean the diode?" I ventured.

"Yes, yes, why you take so long. That is what I said, *disting*, de diode."

The fault was soon put right: we did have a *this thing*!

Bureaucracy is a terrible legacy. What the British colonial masters taught they taught well and the Nigerians, like so many others, were receptive students. This came home to me when I was summoned by a very senior official at the Ministry to provide an explanation for an oil leak which had occurred, since hand-over of the system, at Zaria in the North. The leak had been observed and reported by a trainee technician one year to the day previously. He had reported it, in writing, to the head of shift; he had reported it, in writing, to the head of power maintenance; he had reported it, in writing, to the head of station maintenance, and so on. It had taken 365 days and twelve monthly reports to rise to the top of the pyramid. We investigated and found that an oil seal was defective on a diesel generator.

Although it was a minor fault, having been brought in at the top, we reported back to the top. One year later a memorandum arrived back in Zaria, several sheets thick. Our letter had been supplemented by a cover note at every stage on the way down. When the technician at Zaria went to carry out the instruction on the memo which he received two years after raising the initial report, he was puzzled. There was no oil leak. Of course not, as soon as our engineers had been made aware of the problem they had replaced the seal. Records showed that repairs had been carried out fifty-one weeks earlier.

When there is a quantum uplift in a nation's

infrastructure, contracts very often become interdependent. So it was at Gombe on the spur radio system from Bauchi to Yola. The advent of mains electricity meant that we had to supply a standby-to-mains generator rather than dual diesels. The high voltage step-down transformer was being supplied by others and was on a tight delivery schedule. It duly arrived at Apapa docks and was loaded onto a flat-bed truck. Concern arose over the stability of the load over the rough road surfaces between Apapa and Gombe, a distance of several hundred miles. The order was given to ensure that the transformer must not be able to move on the trailer.

What you ask for is what you get. The transformer arrived at site welded to the trailer bed in the most permanent way imaginable. All efforts to release it failed. The contract schedule was still achievable but the demurrage charges on the trailer were shooting up by the day. Eventually it was decided that the cost was soon going to exceed the value of the trailer and so the decision was made to purchase it. A bigger hole was prepared and the transformer was installed complete with the trailer, forming a very stable plinth!

One of my earliest trips out of the office was to a government department at Oshodi on the north side of Lagos. I accompanied my boss to a formal meeting of some importance. During the session we were served with tea. Very welcome, until I glanced down at my cup to see a huge bluebottle floating on the surface. Worse still, there were no spoons. As I raised my line of sight I noticed the eyes of our host looking into mine and I am sure I detected the slightest vestige of a smile on his silent lips as a surface slick spread around the fly.

The business discussion proceeded while I contemplated my options. Clearly I was not about to receive a replacement cup. Not wishing to consider the recent itinerary of a Lagos fly, I quietly plucked the offending beastie between my thumb and forefinger and went on to sip down the ultra-sweet contents of the cup. My colleague had watched all of this in silent amusement and complemented me on the way home.

"Just trying you out," he said. "Happens to every newcomer. After three years you will just swallow the fly."

Our Finance Manager was a jovial little Irishman from Blackrock. He loved his rugby, scrum-half of course, even in the heat of Lagos and was half way to producing a fifteen of his own. His wife was a cheerful Dublin girl whom I never heard complain about a thing, probably unique among expat wives in Lagos. One evening I got a guffaw out of Pron with a tongue-in-cheek Irish joke.

"How do you confuse an Irishman?"

"No, go on."

"Offer him two shovels and tell him to take his pick."

A week later, Marie cornered me and protested, "Please don't tell Pron any more Irish jokes. He tries to repeat them and always gets them wrong."

"Which one in particular?" I queried.

"This one," she said. "How do confuse an Irishman? Give him two shovels and tell him to take his choice. It was embarrassing. He was the only person in the room laughing."

Pron got his own back on me shortly afterwards. A delightful young lady from the national television service arrived at our door and asked if my wife and I would like to take part, with our daughters, on a TV family quiz programme. This sounded fraught to me and I was very evasive. My wife kept quiet. I asked why she had picked us and was not surprised to hear that we had been recommended by Pron. In the end we agreed to go along to the studio to watch the following week's filming.

We were ushered into front row seats and waited expectantly for the contestants. They turned out to be a British banker and his family up against a Nigerian doctor and his family. I do not recall all the prizes that were up for grabs but I do remember that one was a second-hand paperback book.

Question One (to the Nigerians): "Who is the Head of State of Nigeria?"

Answer: "General Yakubu Gowon," followed by thunderous applause.

Question Two (to the Brits): "Who is the Deputy Minister for Sport in Benue-Plateau State?"

Answer (in hushed tones): "We do not have the faintest idea."

I had seen enough. At the first interval, we gratefully declined the invitation and took our leave.

I mentioned expat. wives. Their tongues could be vicious. The British Wives club was invariably referred to as the Bitches and Witches, with some justification. On one occasion, I was bearded in the Ikoyi Club by the wife of the general manager of one of the prominent British banks.

"I say," she shrilled, "are you the Number One in your company?"

"No," I replied, "as it happens I'm the Number Two."

"Oh, pity," she went on, "we only invite Number Ones to dinner."

From that day since, I have been pleased with the spontaneity of my retort, "Thank Heavens for that!"

Dinner parties were the venues for the exchange of many interesting and humorous accounts. The copious volume of alcohol available eased tongues and relaxed the ears late into the tropical nights.

One of the funniest stories related to one of the more serious events. It wasn't so much the story that was amusing; it was the way that it was told. The local Crown Agent, who was the host, had been a passenger on a Nigerian Airways Fokker Friendship which had crash-landed at Port Harcourt two days previously.

"What is it like to be on a plane that is in trouble?" someone asked.

"Well, it was quite strange actually," he replied in a plummy Surrey accent. "I thought we were coming in rather fast as we touched down. My suspicions were raised when we hopped over the perimeter fence and into a ploughed field. My worst fears were confirmed when a lady, still strapped in her seat, shot down the aisle and wedged in the flight deck doorway. So, I folded up my Daily Telegrarph ."

He didn't get any more out. We were all rolling in our seats convulsed with laughter.

Lagos was visited on a regular schedule by the Elder-

Dempster liner *Aureol* which sailed from Southampton, calling at Tenerife, Banjul, Freetown and Tema on the way down. She always arrived with on-board provisions of apples, celery, grapes and British beer, commodities which were as rare as rocking horse manure in Lagos. It was therefore a coveted privilege to be invited to the Captain's table with one's wife for lunch while *Aureol* was in port. Even though it was the hottest part of the day, no one minded that it was a jacket and tie occasion. All the more room to smuggle the contraband booty of apples and celery ashore afterwards. Goodness knows what port employees thought we had been eating but everyone came off a very different shape from when they had embarked.

My size elevens went right in past the ankle during one *Aureol* lunch. The skipper queried whether I had done much sailing.

"No," I told him innocently, "my last sea trip was on an old tub called the *RMS Seaforth* across the Minch from Kyle of Lochalsh to Stornaway, some fifteen years previously."

His eyes contemplated the table cloth.

"Oh, I see," he demurred in his soft Highland accent, "an old tub was she? I'll let you in on a wee secret. I was the Captain of the *Seaforth* at that time. She was my first command. A lovely wee craft."

I've probably been blacklisted by Caledonian MacBrayne ever since!

After a short time in territory it became obvious that my wife was going to need some wheels of her own. A likely sounding opportunity was passed on to me by a friend in

IBM and I duly made an appointment to visit the house of the vendor on the neighbouring Victoria Island. He turned out to be a Frenchman from Clermont Ferrand. He was the antithesis of the Michelin man, tall, angular, straight black hair and horn-rimmed spectacles, but the Michelin man he was.

After a few pleasantries we got down to discussing his wife's Mini Cooper.

"Eet eez ze very good car," I was told, very seriously. "Eet has always been very well looked after. Eet eez serveeced regularly at ze CFAO."

At this point there was an amazing shriek of laughter from an African grey parrot in a cage behind me.

As I cowered forward, my protagonist leapt to his feet and shouted, "Shut up you stupeed parott!"

Obviously the bird only understood French for it continued to cackle away in its cage.

We resumed our negotiation and eventually concluded the deal at Six Hundred Pounds sterling. On completion we rose from our seats and engaged in a vigorous handshake.

"Da-da-da-daa daa daa daa daa da-da!" shrieked the African grey to the tune of *'La Marseillaise'*.

"I shall kill zis bloody parott!" shouted my host, waving his arms menacingly.

It's strange how friendships strike up. My wife and I went on to become very friendly with the Michelin man and his charming wife, who hailed from Bonn. Our kids also became good friends. He turned out to be not so serious at all, but an outrageously funny man who could take off Monsieur Hulot to a tee and revelled in the sheer joy of living.

Another of our good friendships to evolve in Lagos was that with the resident Raleigh manager, a man with a wicked sense of humour, along the John Cleese lines this time. He also had a keen eye for business. Traffic on Lagos Island had to be seen to be believed. You could often be sat in the same spot for hours waiting for yourself to move in the total gridlock. Our Raleigh man put this to his own advantage by regularly having his driver move onto the end of such a congestion. Having given adjacent drivers sufficient time to work themselves into a lather, he would descend from his car, open the boot and assemble a folding bicycle. Waving to all, he would serenely pedal off to his office, leaving his driver to pick up all the subsequent sales enquiries before bringing back the car.

One of his favourite sales pitches was to ask a group of children, "What do Raleigh make?"

Full of confidence they would reply, jumping up and down in triumph, "Bicycles Sir!"

"No!" he would reply to their consternation. "Raleigh do not make bicycles, they make the **best** bicycles."

Upon which, the kids would clap and cheer, rushing off in all directions to proclaim to the nation, "Raleigh not make de bicycle, dey make de **best** bicycle!"

The Emir of Kano must have been listening. He became the owner of a fully chromium plated model.

Talking of bicycles, I had to laugh during a brown out one night as I halted at a junction with the Awolowa Road. I was aware of something about to move in front of my car but it was dark and it had no lights. Then it passed, a black policeman wearing black clothes on a black bicycle on a pitch black night, shouting defensively, "Honk-honk, honk-honk."

He didn't even have a bell!

Another amusing sight, at least to a European, was that of a man with a bicycle and a wheelbarrow. If I wanted to transport them together, I would put the bicycle in the barrow and push. This man had a much faster mode of transportation; he put the wheelbarrow on his head, mounted the bike and pedalled like fury. Very effective. Try it!

In Nigeria, as with all police forces, many officers acted with great courtesy and efficiency while a few had to be watched all the way, especially as pay day approached. My experience was that most of the trouble that expats got into, with both civil and military police, was of their own making, by not making allowance for communication difficulties or by adopting a superior and arrogant manner. Certainly not in all cases, as I discovered one day when driving in Apapa.

I patiently waited for a gap to appear in the line of traffic on the Wharf roundabout. I waited a long time. Eventually a car stopped and the driver beckoned me in. As soon as I had entered the flow, a military policeman jumped in front of my Land Rover and ordered me to pull over onto the road leading into the Apapa docks. Arriving at my window he accused me of dangerous driving. I knew and he knew that this was false. I told him so. He then told me that this was a very serious offence and I could be sent to jail for a very long time. I told him that, if it was dash that he was after he would be disappointed. He then threatened to take me to his superior officer. I told him that I would be honoured to meet his superior officer and opened the passenger door to let him in.

We duly arrived at the Military Police office in the docks complex. I parked and was ordered to wait in a small ante-room while he reported to his senior officer. Eventually I was invited to enter the office to be welcomed by a clean cut young officer festooned with gold braid.

"Good afternoon, Sir," he said in immaculate English. "What precisely is the problem?"

I explained what had occurred. He looked at me, dolefully shaking his head.

"I am sorry, Sir," he atoned, "we do have this problem from time to time. I realise that your time is vital and costly and that our Government does not invite you here to be messed around in this way. Please accept my sincere apology and wait outside."

I thanked him warmly, stepped back into the ante-room and closed the door.

Seconds later I thought the roof was going to leave the building. The rogue MP was on the receiving end of the loudest verbal shellacking, in Yoruba, that I had heard since my days at Catterick. Eventually he emerged red faced and shaking and told me I could go. I exited and climbed into my Land Rover, turned round and made to move away.

Before I could do so, over came the villain of the piece and shouted at me, "You will give me a job with your company."

"Not on your Nelly," I responded, "you do not have the right qualifications. Would you like a lift back to the roundabout?"

"No, I am not going to de roundabout."

A more amusing incident came to pass one evening after several hours of snooker at the Ikoyi Club. Four of our senior managers were out from the UK for a series of contract negotiations and were seeking some innocent relaxation. Come half past midnight we were starting to wilt and decided to call it a day. We set off in my 1600E to drop each of them off at his appointed abode, thinking that was it for the day. No such luck!

When pulling off the road and slowing down to stop outside the first house, there was a terrific thump on the rear near-side wing. Leaping out to inspect, I found a severe dent, missing the rear passenger window by inches, and below it, lying on the gravel, a weighty looking boulder.

"What in the name ?" I started.

Out of the palm trees came a piercing female voice.

"Move de car or I will throw another stone."

Meantime two of my passengers made a bolt for the gate of the property as if ten thousand devils were after them. There stood before us a wild eyed woman with matted hair, normally taken to indicate an advanced state of mental disarray.

That was no place to hang around and reason so we drove off without further ado. Spotting two policemen standing on a roundabout, I stopped by them and indicated the damage.

"Were you stationary at de time?" one asked.

"Yes," I replied, "I had pulled off the road to allow two passengers to get out."

"Den it is not our concern. We are de moving traffic police. You will report dis incident to de Ikoyi Police Station."

Confirming that my colleagues were happy to go along with this, we drove round to the designated station.

It was still hot, a light was beaming from the small building surrounded by palms and two clients were leaving as we entered.

"What is your name and address?" I was challenged before I had even reached the desk.

Feeling like a criminal already, I duly spouted out the requisite details. The enquirer was a burly middle-aged sergeant who looked as if he was having one of those nights when nothing goes right. Two constables were horizontal on the floor behind him, fast asleep and clearly not giving him much assistance.

"What is de problem?"

"Well, Sergeant, we were stopping outside Number Twelve Mobilaji Johnson Way   "

"What of dis Mobilaji Johnson Way?"

"It was formerly called Kingsway, Sergeant. The State Government changed the name yesterday."

"Eh-heh! Nobody is telling me dis."

There had been public notices throughout the press, on radio and television and, after all, it was in his parish.

"Never mind. Continue wid de description of de crime."

I continued to relate how the mad woman had pitched a

boulder at my car.

"What was de number of de house in dis King   .er Mobilaji Johnson Way?"

"Number Twelve Sergeant."

He looked relieved , responding triumphantly, "Den it is not de concern of dis police station. Our authority finishes at de Number Fourteen. You will report dis matter to de Awolowa Road Police Station."

I could see the strategy and had no intention of becoming a ping-pong ball.

"Tomorrow morning, Sergeant, the Chief of Police for the whole of Nigeria will travel in his official car along Mobilaji Johnson Way from his house to his office. If the mad woman throws a stone at his car and damages it, I shall say, "Good morning, Chief, exactly the same thing happened to me during the night and I reported it to Ikoyi Police Station, but the duty sergeant refused to take action."

Perspiration appeared on the sergeant's brow.

"No, no, dat is not good for me, I will take action!"

He leaned over one of the snoozing constables, giving him a hefty but fruitless kick as he did so.

Two coughs to clear the throat then, "Testing, testing, testing, one, two tree, four, five."

Two more coughs, much more authoritative this time.

"Dis am de Base to de Mobile One, come in de Mobile One. Over"

Silence was the deafening response.

I glanced round towards my two colleagues. Keith had had to step outside to relieve himself, otherwise he would have peed himself laughing. John was leaning against the open door frame, Gaulloise in hand, whistling the theme to *Z Cars*.

Undeterred, the sergeant pressed on.

"Ugh-hugh! He is sleeping."

Click.

"Dis am de Base to de Mobile Two, come in de Mobile Two. Over."

Again, silence.

"Come in de Mobile Two, dis am de Base, wake up Mobile Two."

A strange noise emanated from the receiver, sounding like a donkey in distress.

"Eeaaghhh .Dis am de Mobile One to de Base. Come in de Base. Over."

"Eh-heh! You were sleeping Mobile One. Dat is not my concern. You will proceed to de scene of de crime at Number Twelve Mobilaji Johnson Way."

Interruption.

"What of dis Mobilaji Johnson Way, Sergeant?"

Back thundered the exasperated sergeant, "You are de fool, it was formerly called de Kingsway, you should know dis ting!!!"

"Sorry, Sergeant."

"You will proceed to de scene of de crime and liaise wid de European man who was attacked by de mad woman who throw de stone at his car. Over and out."

"Roger, Roger, over and out."

By now it was approaching two o'clock in the morning. In for a penny, in for a pound we agreed. Rather than stop outside Number Twelve where a renewed attack was a high possibility, I drew up on the verge outside Number Fourteen. It was very dark and very quiet. John had worked his way through two Gaulloises before the first lights appeared behind us.

"This must be him," we agreed, by now wanting to speed up the proceedings.

No luck. A beaten up Toyota Corolla droned past us and into the distance. Two more cars appeared and disappeared. We were all getting restless and ready for some shut-eye when a young chap staggered past, stooping under the weight of a back-pack. It was difficult to discern in the almost total darkness but I was sure I detected the glint of an antenna sticking out of the back-pack

"Excuse me," I called cautiously, "are you Mobile One?"

"Who are you?" he asked, spinning round, startled out of his skin and all but falling under the centrifugal force of the back-pack.

"I am the European with whom you are to liaise."

"Dat is not right. I have to liaise wid de European outside de Number Twelve."

"Aha, but if I stop outside Number Twelve the mad woman will throw another stone at my car."

This agreed we alighted and walked cautiously towards the palm trees outside Number Twelve. At first there was no sound or movement. She must have been sleeping.

Then a wild shriek, "Go away or I will attack you!"

Our policeman friend, retreating three paces, was visibly shaken.

"I de police. Why you throw de stone at de car of dis

man?"

She scowled, "It is after midnight. All de Europeans should be in bed. I not throw de stone, I play ball wid de stone. I throw de ball in de air and de European drive de car under de ball."

Our gendarme plucked up courage.

"I am arresting you for de crime of causing de criminal damage."

She glowered and cringed, "You keep away from me. I am de spirit, not de human. I will put de curse on you, you cannot arrest de spirit."

Joe Ninety was totally flummoxed.

"She is de spirit, Sir, I cannot arrest de spirit."

Keith intervened, "Is that what you will put in your report to the sergeant?"

"No, Sir, I will call for de army?"

With that Mobile One whipped out his portable radio, conferred with the sergeant and informed us that the army was on its way. The army responded at frightening speed, so fast that I suspect they had been watching us from Number Ten. The first soldier called on all his training, seized the initiative and stepped towards the mad woman, Lee-Enfield cocked and ready.

"You are under arrest!"

The mad woman was undeterred.

"I am not de human being, I am de spirit. If you shoot me, I will put de curse on you."

The soldier replaced his safety catch.

"How can you prove dat you are de spirit?"

Whether they understood her response I will never know

but her erudition belied her wanton appearance.

"I lived and died many years ago. I was de servant at de court of de European King Louis."

"Which one?" asked John disingenuously.

"De Fourteenth," she replied in a subdued, almost confidential tone.

Conferring amongst ourselves, John, Keith and I agreed that this learned lady deserved a second chance. She was looking smarter by the minute than any of her uniformed interrogators.

"Perhaps it is a matter for the Awolowa Road Police Station," I ventured, "they have a more senior officer on duty."

Smiles lit up the faces of the soldiers and Mobile One. They were off the hook.

"Dat is de best plan, Sir, you report it to de Awolowa Road Duty Officer. Good night, Sir. Thank you, Sir."

Suddenly we were alone with the not-so-mad woman.

"Good night, lady, we are going home."

She regarded us with a knowing smile, "Good night Sirs, you not come here again after de midnight."

It was 4.20 a.m. when I turned back the sheets to creep into bed. My wife stirred but did not open her eyes.

"Where have you been till this time?" seemed a reasonable question.

"I'll tell you in the morning, you'll never believe me if I tell you now."

The following day we were unable to drive along King sorry, Mobilaji Johnson Way on our way to the Ikoyi Club. The road was being resurfaced and there was a mighty kerfuffle going on outside Number Twelve. It later transpired that the madwoman had taken exception to the road gang's intrusion on to her piece of land and had lobbed a boulder at the driver of the steam roller. They had retaliated by turning the tar sprayer onto her, covering her from head to toe in hot steaming tar. Sad, sad, sad, we all agreed, but it did add conviction to my explanation to my wife.

Personal shopping was a necessary evil if you wanted to get the right goods at the right price. Sending ones domestic staff was always a lottery and invariably the total price amounted to the exact amount of money that they had been given.

There was always a shortage of at least one basic commodity, be it flour, sugar, beer or whatever and one had to depend on the bush telegraph to find out what was where. At one time the only stock of beer we could locate in Nigeria was held by the brothers at the Catholic Mission in Makurdi, halfway across the country. A bulk order was placed and delivered by our field staff. The lucky recipients suddenly became very popular in Lagos.

Change was a really niggling problem, especially in the supermarkets. One would fill a shopping trolley to the gunwales, queue for an hour at the check-out, proffer a wad of notes only to be told, "Sorry, no change."

This happened so often as to be more than a coincidence. Totally frustrated, having spent so long already in the store, most people would just cut their losses and leave. Occasionally however, a determined expat wife would abandon her overloaded trolley and walk out telling the hapless cashier to put the stock back on the shelves herself. This would cause ructions, especially just before closing time.

I got myself into an awkward spot in Kingsway Store through trying out my sense of humour on a cashier who clearly functioned on a different wavelength. Approaching the till with two beautifully carved wooden goblets, I enquired after the price of these egg cups.

"They are not egg cups," I was informed stiffly.

"Perhaps they are egg cups for the ostrich egg," I ventured.

"They are not egg cups," she reaffirmed brusquely.

Seeing that I was on a loser, I conceded.

"OK, I am sorry, they are not egg cups, they are goblets. I will buy two."

"You are not allowed to buy them. You will use them for egg cups."

She was adamant. I did not get them. I had to send my daughter back later to effect the purchase.

No one could fault Kingsway for trying. Their British General Manager tried to import a consignment of grapes from Europe. He was summoned to Apapa docks and asked to explain what they were.

"Oh, they are grapes," he explained to the Customs officer, "they are a fruit."

"They are not allowed into Nigeria," was the firm decision. "We have plenty of grapefruit in Nigeria."

Nor were they. Not even healthy dash could persuade him that grape fruit was not grapefruit.

Dash was a very significant lubricant. A few well placed

Naira could move mountains. Refusal to dash could render the simple impossible. The airport was a good starting point. It was amazing how lost luggage would suddenly be found, how a passport irregularity would suddenly become acceptable or access to a restricted area would magically be granted. First time arrivals were fair game to Immigration, Customs, the Army, baggage handlers and taxi drivers alike. It cost a prominent English bishop the equivalent of Fifty Pounds in dash between leaving his aircraft and arriving in his Lagos hotel room, and he was wearing his ecclesiastical robes. What chance a mere mortal!

I swallowed heavily when my mother-in-law announced that she would be visiting us in Lagos. Not that she was not welcome, she was, but the thought of her negotiating the hazards of the airport terrified me. Taking up position outside the restricted arrival area, I politely asked the soldier barring my way if I could proceed to meet my passenger.

"No! It is forbidden area except for passengers," he told me firmly.

"But I am meeting an old lady, my mother," I pleaded.

"You are not allowed," he said irritably.

"But she is a very old, weak lady,"

I tried again, this time presenting my passport with a ten Naira note inside.

"Ah, you must take care of de sick old lady," he said nodding me through.

I met her just in time to interpret the barely intelligible gibberish of an overworked Immigration officer. No problem there. *Mirabile dictu*, her suitcases were available and intact too. Not wishing to imagine what might be inside them I parted company with another Five Naira as I informed the Customs man "Nothing to declare."

Cases chalked, I proceeded blithely past my military friend guarding the door, my forty-nine year old mother-in-law tripping athletically along in close attendance.

"Goodnight, Corporal and thank-you."

He grinned knowingly back at me and said, "Not very old, not very weak, Sir. Goodnight."

"He was a nice young man," said Mum innocently.

If only she had known what might have been!

Used sensibly, dash was a good system of reward for small services rendered. But it was abused, naturally. The Americans had no compunction over paying several times the accepted rate which made life very difficult for the rest. The recipients started to get greedy and dash was demanded where it should not have been necessary.

It was particularly frustrating to arrive at the counter of a government office, say for a driving licence application form, after several hot, sticky hours in traffic and nowhere to park, to be told, "No forms, de stock is finished. You will come back tomorrow."

And the next day and the next day after that, until you were prepared to bring out your wallet when the stock would suddenly be replenished.

A young engineer from Dumfries, on his first overseas trip, offered a lobby porter at the Eko Holiday Inn a ten kobo tip one evening. The poor chap looked at it incredulously, thrust out his arm and sighed, "You hold on to it, Sir, you might need it."

It was the one and only time I saw a dash or tip refused.

The previous evening, the same engineer had seen one of the ladies who hide in the bushes around the Ikoyi Hotel pressing her favours on me.

As, rejected, she turned away, he said to me, "Your friend seems like a nice girl," and before I could warn him otherwise, he had offered her a drink.

It cost him Sixty Naira to get rid of her once he discovered her profession.

The house boys, known in Nigeria as stewards, and some times assisted by a "small boy", unconsciously created a lot of humour and no doubt had a good laugh at the families whom they served. A Northumbrian friend became so frustrated at his own dinner parties with the constant shuttle of his steward and small boy between the kitchen and the dining room, via the lounge, that he had a serving hatch built into the wall. Having explained that its purpose was to allow the serving of food directly from the kitchen to the dining room he settled back to talk with his guests. His attention was aroused by one dish, one arm and one foot appearing simultaneously through the hatch. Instead of passing the dishes to each other, the steward and small boy were going to take it in turns to climb through the hatch en route to and from table

At the same house, on the occasion of his daughter's christening, my friend had overseen the preparation of a most succulent roast pig.

Eyeing it up ruefully, immediately prior to its being served to table, he said to the steward, "It needs something extra, Sunday. When you serve it, serve it with an apple for mouth and parsley behind the ears."

Sunday duly obliged. There was no change to the porker when it arrived but Sunday had an apple in his mouth and a sprig of parsley behind each of his ears!

Our own steward, a former schoolteacher from Owerri, was excellent. He was also very tactful. I was aware, during one of our dinner parties, that he was listening to the conversation. One of the guests had just related a chilling account of how, during the Mau Mau uprising in Kenya, a Kikuyu house boy had killed all the members of the European family for which he worked. There followed a short silence.

"You wouldn't do that to us, would you Tony?"

"No sir, I would kill the family next door."

Pause.

"Their steward would kill you."

There is honour and loyalty among scoundrels!

Dinner parties were very popular often preceding an evening's bridge. Some played serious bridge, some sensible bridge and others just to pass the time while they nattered. My wife and I were engaged with a couple of Edinburgh friends, late one night, in the sensible variety, when there was an ominous crash outside and the lounge became floodlit by a pair of glaring headlights. We had all had a bit to drink but were still lucid, which was more than could be said of the incumbent of the car outside. He had left the Awolowa Road at some speed, crossed the footpath, cleared the storm drain and crashed through the six foot panelled fence onto the front lawn. Two bleary eyes were rolling round in a very inebriated head.

"Nice of you to drop in," said our host.

The driver was not apparently hurt but was totally confused. The back seat of his car was laden with Campari bottles, all full.

"Having a party?"

"I am a school teacher," burbled the driver. "My wife has given birth to a daughter and we celebrate."

Trying to obtain any details for insurance purposes was not a realistic proposition, so we merely noted the registered number of the car. We were struggling to heave the vehicle back onto level ground when my wife let out a mortified groan.

"Ugh! My leg's going warm," she burst out in disgust, "he's widdling down my leg."

Such was the farce of the event that even that seemed funny and we all fell about with laughter. Eventually we managed to reposition the car on the road pointing in the right direction, congratulated our visitor on his newly achieved fatherhood and waved him on his way. He was last seen disappearing the wrong way round the Kingsway roundabout.

Together with some English friends we decided to spend Christmas 1974 in Lome, Togo. Just as we were about to leave, along the road came our Company's contracted signwriter, Lincoln Arts, dragging a turkey on a rope.

"Power, Sir. Long life to Madam. A Christmas gift for your family," he offered generously.

I gratefully accepted the reluctant looking fowl and exchanged pleasantries with this eternally cheerful gentleman who had walked some miles with his feathered friend in tow. Fortunately for the turkey it was about to gain a reprieve over Christmas. I called Tony from the stewards' quarters, gave him some cash and told him to tie the bird to a tree and feed it until we returned from Togo.

After a delightful holiday, during which we drove through the old slave shipping port of Badagri and on through Cotoneau in what was then still called Dahomey, we returned to find a very sombre looking Tony, chin on chest and clearly too embarrassed to speak.

"Did you and your family enjoy Christmas?" I asked tentatively.

"Yes, Sir," he replied in a very subdued voice.

"And the mass, was it uplifting?" I went on, wanting him to identify his problem.

He was well paid relative to his peers, he was well treated, the atmosphere in the stewards' quarters was cheerful when we left, I was at a loss. Perhaps he had suffered a bereavement.

"And the turkey, how is the turkey, Tony? Eating well?"

Pause.

"It is dead Sir, it not eat, it get sick and die, Sir. When we go to chop it, it is full of maggot, Sir."

Relieved that he had discovered that before it reached our oven, I asked how he had disposed of the foul fowl.

"I put it in de garbage bin, Sir."

I glanced towards our bin, wondering what the multiplication rate of maggots might be in the hot, humid equatorial climate. I need not have worried.

"Not your bin, Sir, de bin of de family next door."

Trusting that our Dutch neighbour did not personally use or inspect his dustbin, I thanked Tony for his good sense and initiative, gave him small dash to buy some extra food for his wife and baby and retreated indoors for a relieving bottle of Star beer.

Just going back to Togo for a minute, what a lovely little oasis it turned out to be. Still with a strong German influence, evidenced by the regular appearance at the airport of the blue and gold of Lufthansa and the first class restaurants, including my favourite, the Alt Muenchen, it had a wonderfully relaxed air. The French had taken over the political reins from the Germans long before independence and exhibited a much more equitable relationship with the Togolese than would ever be found in a former British colony. Pert young French girls served alongside their African sisters in the boulangerie. In the lift of our hotel one morning I came across a French mechanic, oil up to his elbows, laughing and joking and sharing cigarettes with an equally jovial Togolese. We were just not used to that.

If you wanted to study the relationship between the British and their Commonwealth cousins, a visit to our field depot at Oshodi would have been a good starting point. Oshodi was where all the imported equipment was marshalled prior to its despatch by road to sites across the length and breadth of Nigeria It was also the repair centre for equipment and vehicles. The ingenuity of the Nigerian mechanics employed there was of a very high order indeed. How they kept the fleet of a hundred or so Land Rovers, trucks and cars on the road with write-offs limited to single figures was amazing, given the road conditions, the indiscipline of the traffic, the climatic conditions and the crazy handling of the drivers.

The relationship between our expatriate staff and the locally engaged employees was very robust indeed. Many changes of personnel were necessary before the work force could be described as honest and hard working, but once the local lads had earned their spurs their was mutual respect and dependability of a very high order. It was quite clear that the Nigerians did not care for soft or incompetent expat managers. They liked to know where they stood, that the manager knew what he was talking about and that he was true to his word. How rough the diamond did not matter, so long as it was a diamond. There was a lot of give and take and a lot of good-natured banter.

"Give us the job and we'll finish the tools!"
read a banner on the maintenance centre wall.

"We can fuck up a steel ball!"
read another. But without the integrity and cohesion of a support force such as we had, execution of the nation-wide field project would have been downright impossible.

From where I sat in an air-conditioned office on Lagos Island, a lot of it looked very unfair at times but the chaps on the ground at Oshodi would tell a far different tale, I am sure.

On one occasion, in the rainy season, it was reported that goods were mysteriously going missing from Oshodi Depot during the night. Mysterious because the compound was very securely fenced and padlocked, with a team of night-watchmen (watchnights, or *magadi*s, as they were called) strategically positioned. We eventually discovered that the goods were being floated out through a culvert to a team waiting outside the perimeter fence.

In another instance, hundreds of yards of sheathed cable was fed out from its storage drums through a small hole in the wire mesh fence, eventually to be burned to get at its copper core.

We were not the only ones to fall prey to such initiative. A Japanese company buried several miles of cable between Ijebu-Ode and Benin City. When they came to switch on the system for performance testing, nothing happened. Taking to the road to pinpoint the fault, they were astounded to find that as they had laid the cable, some bright sparks had come along behind them, coiling it up and making off with it. Same purpose, for the copper.

Even more astounding was what happened to the electricity system being installed by a British company between Aba and Calabar. High tension wires were slung between pylons along the length of the route in the time honoured way. Come switch on, same thing, no circuit. This time they found that not only the wire was missing, but the pylons as well. They were all found on Aba market. The pylons had been sawn up to construct bed frames and the wire had been destranded and cut to make coat hangers! I am told you can buy anything you care to name on the markets at Aba and Onitsha; I am prepared to believe it! They are the Harrods of West Africa.

My own first trip to the old East Central State was not without incident. It had been agreed that a public relations exercise might smooth the way for Government works in what had been until recently a turbulent war zone. A film show was arranged followed by a cocktail party. The guests formed a wide cross section of dignitaries from the area including academics, politicians and business leaders. The film, showing similar work carried out in Australia, generated a lot of interest and enthusiasm and was followed by a lively question and answer session. Hosts and guests mingled well at the cocktail party.

Although the affair was essentially a management function, we had a few field engineers working around Enugu at the time and it would have been churlish and tasteless not to have invited them along. The trouble was the disparity in social behaviour. Some of our field lads were pretty down to earth and prone to calling a spade a bloody shovel. My sensors were alerted therefore when I spotted a particularly direct Geordie installer in animated conversation with the State Minister for Education.

As I drew within earshot the chat was proceeding along the following lines.

"So how long have you been in Nigeria?" enquired the Minister in a polished Oxbridge accent.

"Aboot fave year," was the reply.

"You must really enjoy our country to have remained here so long," intoned the Minister.

Then, what I had feared.

"Way aye man, the North's OK. Doon in the Sooth-West you've got your Yoruba; he's as thick as pig shit and argumentative with it. Over here in the East you've got your Ibo. He's a lot more clever but he's as cunning as a cartload of monkeys. Up in the North you've got your good old Hausa. He's happy all the time and doesn't give a stuff about any thing, he's the man for me."

"Oh, really," stammered the politician, somewhat bemused, "what an interesting analysis of our country's cultural problems."

Pretending not to have heard, I wheeled the Minister away and changed the subject.

Looking back over his shoulder, he commented, "A very colourful colleague you have there."

"Oh, excellent worker," I enthused. "Loves being in Nigeria."

The opposite end of the social spectrum was the bar of the Presidential Hotel in Enugu. I had been enticed there by the promise of ice cold draught lager served in pewter tankards. The lager was excellent but the mould and verdigris nestling in the lower reaches of the tankards was off-putting to say the least. The tables were large and rough hewn and the lighting was almost non-existent but the company was cheerful and the talk was ribald.

We were all well into the mellow stage when I felt an interference below table level at the front of my trousers. Peering down into the gloom I could just make out the whites of a pair of eyes and the glint of smiling teeth.

Recoiling quickly and protecting my zip, I cried, "What's that?"

As what appeared to be a very young ebony teenage girl grinned out of the murky depths, one of our lads exhorted,

"Go on, she's offering you a free sample. I'll have it if you don't want it."

"You're welcome!" I gracefully conceded.

The company house that night was like the Gorbals on Hogmanay. When paying a visit to the toilet we did not know who we were going to bump into or step on next. Half the ladies of Enugu must have been staying there. Sleep was a forlorn ambition. How much beer had been consumed that evening I shudder to think but it did not put the residents off their breakfast.

At six-thirty the following morning, one of the aerial erectors rent the air, bellowing, "Steward!" followed by the urgent patter of bare feet.

"Yessir?"

"Is that sun over the yard-arm yet?"

"Yessir."

"Well where's my bloody Star?"

"Your Star beer is coming Sir, four bottles."

Phew, oh for the peace of Lagos.

Further East the commissioning of the radio transmission system from Calabar to Ogoja was taking place. The rains had been particularly heavy and the rivers streaming down from the Cameroon Highlands into the Cross River were in spate. Ikom Bridge had been seriously damaged enforcing a long detour for road travellers making for Ogoja. One of our engineers had made the detour but had under-estimated the amount of fuel required to compensate for the extra distance. He almost made it back to Calabar but his Land Rover ran out of fuel outside the military barracks on the edge of town.

He was immediately surrounded by soldiers informing him that it was a sensitive area and he could not stop there.

The sun was fierce with the temperature in the high nineties. The vehicle was too heavy to push and he was not the strongest of individuals. In fact he was quite skinny with a cherubic face and was fair game for his tormentors. They decreed that his punishment would be to sit on the bonnet of his Land Rover for one hour. It would have been searing hot had it been merely standing still in the direct sunlight. After a round trip to Ogoja it was near on boiling. The poor wretch survived, but not without extensive blistering to his backside and legs.

My safaris northwards tended to be less eventful than those to the East. They were not totally devoid of humour though. On a tour of the Mid West, I was amazed to find a telephone exchange where the floors compared admirably with those in Catterick Camp on inspection day. Our man in charge was a studious young chap with a double barrelled name. The bush was certainly not his chosen environment and I was told that he regularly undertook a thirty mile round trip to Akure to use the toilet. Squatting behind a coconut palm, as was the wont of his colleagues, was not for him.

At Oshogbo, our installers were having a torrid time with the mains electricity supply. While I was there it blew yet again. We opened a control switch box to find that two lizards had caused the fault by hatching out of their eggs inside the box and being welded across the switch contacts. The two broken eggs were found when the switch was dismantled. As one joker remarked, the original crocodile clip.

On my first visit to Ibadan, I decided to drive myself in

order to gain some navigating skills. My first view of the town was from the crest of a hill on the southern outskirts. Stretching before me was the biggest sea of shanty dwellings I have encountered, rusting corrugated iron roof tops as far as the eye could see, and there in the distance, buried in this mass of corrosion, was the radio tower rising above the station to which I was heading. So much for navigation! I stopped and walked over to a taxi driver, taking his siesta in his cab with his knuckles trailing the ground and his horny, brown feet perched on the steering wheel. As I approached he came to life.

"You see that tower?" I gestured. "Will you take me there?"

"Of course," he replied opening the rear door.

"No," I said, "I have my own car."

He looked at me as if I had climbed down out of the trees.

"I do not know how to get there. You go in your taxi and I will follow you in my car. I will give you half of the fare now and the balance when we arrive there. How is that?"

He scratched his head and scrutinised me for half a minute.

"OK," he said eventually, "I never understand you crazy Europeans."

It is a good ploy. It works.

It was good to get out of Lagos occasionally. As with all big cities they become claustrophobic after a while. I was fortunate in having the opportunity. My wife and daughters spent every single day of 1973 within the city.

One pleasure was to stop at the villages along the way,

119

buy some fruit (at ridiculously low prices), chat with the local people and take some refreshment. This was the real Nigeria, I always felt, away from the greed and squalor encountered so often in the cities. I was fascinated one lunch-time, when in the company of some local farmers in an inn at Ilaro, between Lagos and Abeokuta, to find the conversation revolving around the weather and the state of the crops. It was exactly the scenario one would have expected in deepest rural England.

Internal flights were always a lottery in my book. Either the aircraft had gone technical or some political or military VIP had commandeered the plane. Harmattan over Kano, Colonel X has to take his girl friend back to Port Harcourt, you name it there was always a reason for a flight to be late or cancelled.

At that time it was possible to use the Lagos - Kano - Rome Alitalia flight for the domestic sector if seats were available. One engineer decided to do just that as he had done many times before. Dress code was not something that bothered working expat engineers in the torrid heat and he travelled in his usual rig of cotton T-shirt, shorts and flip-flops. Sadly, the Harmattan had descended from the Sahara and the flight from Lagos overflew Kano. He confessed that he had never felt such a prat as he did at Rome Airport dressed as he was in January with three inches of snow outside.

Late one afternoon I was dropped by our Kaduna personnel at Zaria Airport for a flight back to Lagos. At the time Kaduna Airport was undergoing runway strengthening. Zaria was smaller and could only handle reduced payloads. When I checked in there was absolute pandemonium going on in the departure area. Two flights had landed, both going to Lagos, one calling in at Ibadan on the way. Both were overbooked and were already loaded to the revised capacity. The poor old checking clerk was under siege, everyone shouting at once, arms flying in all directions and all trying to push to the front.

I stood well clear of this chaos and happened to look down at two documents on the desk on which I was leaning. Not only were they the passenger manifests for the two flights, I spotted the name of an acquaintance from the Ikoyi Club, not on one of the manifests but on both. Ignoring the fellow under siege, I wandered over to the check-in desk and pointed out this anomaly to an alert looking young clerk.

"This is a very serious error, Sir," he acknowledged, taking the manifests gratefully.

"Do you know which aircraft he is on.?"

"Oh, yes," I lied between my teeth, "he always takes the Ibadan flight on a Friday night. It is usually less congested. Which reminds me, if he is on the Ibadan flight, there is an empty seat on the direct flight."

The clerk was too relieved to argue.

"You are correct, Sir, you may have it but you must carry your own baggage to the aircraft."

That was no problem, I only had an overnight bag. I shot out of a side door like a greyhound from a trap and sprinted across the tarmac. By the time the jostling crowd realised what was happening, the clerk had radioed the aircraft, the doors were open and I was on board.

As I took my seat, the gentleman sitting next to me said in studied English tones, "My, my, you have worked up a lather."

I glanced through the cascade of perspiration. It was my acquaintance from the Ikoyi Club.

To meet with misfortune while out driving on one's own was always a potential hazard. Not that one would be on one's own for long, Instant-Rent-A-Crowd saw to that. In the city or in the deepest bush, any event involving a European could be relied on to draw the crowds. Whether in the right or in the wrong, the avoidance of becoming embroiled in a roadside argument was imperative. Nigerian traders first coined the term *palaver*; the Yoruba made an art form out of it.

On one occasion while driving myself across the Ijora Causeway in Lagos, my car decided that it had had enough. Before I could apply the hand brake a hundred bodies had emerged from the open ends of a stack of newly imported water pipes and already had the bonnet up.

"I am de mechanic, I will help you Sir," emerged simultaneously from a hundred pairs of lips.

Seizing the initiative, as one had to do, I bearded the biggest roughest looking individual I could see and informed the crowd, "This man is my mechanic."

Sound move. He obviously had respect for whatever reason and the others fell back.

"Here is de problem, Sir, de rotor arm is missing."

It had clearly been there prior to the arrival of the mob. I dashed him substantially to guard the vehicle while I took a taxi back to my office and handed the matter over to our

Nigerian driver. He reappeared two hours later with the car intact.

"Someone had cut your fuel pipe, Sir," he reliably informed me.

The trick employed was to cut the fuel pipe of a parked vehicle close to the petrol tank and stuff the silver paper from a cigarette packet into the end of the pipe. This allowed sufficient fuel to drive a few hundred yards whereupon the car would stop and the "mechanics" would be lying in wait to offer their expensive services.

It is always a wise move, when selecting a fleet of vehicles for a contract, to observe what cars the local taxi drivers use. Peugeot and Toyota were the in brands at that time; purchasing a fleet of Triumphs or Rovers might have been very patriotic but could leave the hapless driver with a multitude of problems in the procurement of spare parts. One chap taking no risk was an eminent lawyer who lived on Ikoyi Island. Not only did he purchase a Rolls-Royce, he purchased a complete second identical model in knock down form for use as spares for the first. Where did I go wrong?

Nigeria in the mid-seventies was on the crest of an oil boom. There was nothing it could not afford. Maintenance had never really been in fashion but now it was erased from the lexicon. If something goes wrong, throw it away and buy a new one. Be it tractors from Europe, locomotives from Canada or generators from Japan, the wastage was wanton and prolific.

Cement was being shipped in for the building and road construction industries faster than the world's merchant shipping fleets could cope. Long since abandoned Greek tubs were being put back to sea with no hope whatsoever of obtaining a seaworthy certificate and were being abandoned after delivery along the West African coast. Some set solid and sank as the sea seeped in.

Their was a floating city of vessels anchored off Apapa on which all manner of bestialities were taking place, rape, murder, suicide and piracy to name but a few. At times, as seen from the Ikoyi Hotel's Atlantic Towers Restaurant, there were more lights at sea than on land. The boom could not last and people who had tasted riches fell back to rags. It might have been better if the country had never risen beyond its agro-economy, times when everyone had something, even if a little, and greed was not the driving force.

In spite of the huge oil revenues the electricity and water supply utilities were never able to get their respective acts together. Power outages, known in Nigeria as brown-outs, were initially random then later phased on a rota basis, with the random outages thrown in as extras. Hour after hour without electricity, and hence air-conditioning, was a nightmare in the all embracing humidity of Lagos, particularly for couples with young children.

Even more distressing were the water cut-offs. Not so frequent, but of longer duration when they did occur, they were paralysing. Unable to wash self or clothes, people grew exasperated at their own filth and discomfort. If I had to make a choice, I would sacrifice the power any day rather than the water. Unfortunately for many, the water supply was dependent on an electric pump to get the water to the header tank. This led to a boom in generator sales which soon exhausted stocks. Whatever you tried there was always another problem waiting.

Most disconcerting was the constant threat of disease. Personal hygiene had to be kept at the highest order at all times, prophylactic medicines had to be taken with unerring regularity and jabs had to be kept up to date. These included polio, typhoid, tetanus, cholera, yellow fever, smallpox, all of which made your arm feel like a colander, not to mention the dear old gamma globulin shot which left you feeling that you had a golf ball buried in one cheek of your backside. All of this did not prevent my wife and younger daughter falling host to the female anopheles mosquito. Fiona, my eldest daughter, had successfully survived meningitis a year before we went to Nigeria. That was a trauma I never wanted repeated, now here we were with two cases of malaria. Seeing ones family in such pain and distress is much worse than suffering oneself. In that environment it was agonising.

Later I was also to go under, in my case with relapsing fever. I was informed by the Institute of Tropical Diseases in St.Pancras that the nearest differential diagnosis of that particular disease at that time was in Addis Ababa, but that was of scant consolation to me as I lay drugged and blindfolded against the light. My head felt as though it was in a galvanised bucket on which someone was playing the *1812 Overture* with a sledgehammer. No sooner had I improved than I would go under again, hence the name, relapsing fever. After six relapses I was more paranoid when feeling well and anticipating a relapse than during the attack itself, when I was hardly conscious of anything other than the excruciating pain. Nevertheless I would have gone through all of that again sooner than seeing my wife and daughter suffering with malaria.

"What am I doing," I kept on asking myself, "bringing them here and subjecting them to this?"

The only other time I suffered pain in any way approaching that was when I was selected to play for the Ikoyi Club at tennis against a team representing Ibadan. My opponent was an athletically built Nigerian Airways captain who was not at all distressed by the heat. I played regularly from four o'clock onwards, when the power had gone out of the sun, but this day we went on court at noon. Man, did I suffer. By the start of the third set my legs had turned to jelly, my head was pounding like a cannon and my clothes were as heavy as lead with perspiration. At that point discretion got the better part of valour and I retired. I was gasping for a drink but everything was iced and there was a high risk of stomach cramp, so I sat and sipped and suffered, and suffered, and suffered.

Apart from illness, in all the time while we were in Nigeria there were only two incidents where I felt genuine fear for the safety of my family. Both occurred in the early stage of our first tour.

We had spent a most enjoyable morning at the Surulere home of a business acquaintance of my father-in-law, an automotive engineer who had dined at our home in England shortly before our departure. I recall that he had incredible difficulty with blackberry seeds, with which he was totally unfamiliar, getting stuck under his dentures.

Anyway, he had given us a fine lunch and to our embarrassment had generously filled the boot of our car with fruit, bananas, grapefruit, pineapples and coconuts. From Surulere, we had arranged to meet some British friends at the Airport Hotel swimming pool.

Driving at walking speed through a market on the congested Agege Motor Road, we were spotted by a group of young men who clearly resented our presence. As they rained down blows with iron bars and cycle chains on the roof of our car, I decided to get the hell out of there and there was only one way. Up on the footpath we went, behind a telegraph pole, through some stalls, headlights full on and horn blaring. A path miraculously cleared in the startled crowd, sufficient for us to get far enough away to relax and return to normality. I dread to think what would have become us if they had managed to open the doors or break the windows. We had heard of cases of rubber necklacing where people were circled from shoulders to feet in old tyres, doused in petrol and set alight. People who can do that are capable of anything.

The second incident was at our apartment on Ikoyi Island. Traders called regularly at expat houses hawking anything from art to furniture. Usually they would take the tenth no for an answer or were elated to effect a modest sale. As soon as this one entered our lounge I knew that, this time, I had let in a wrong 'un. A surly individual with a heavily scarred face and the physique of Mike Tyson, he brought with him some tables with supports carved in the shape of elephants, one large oval table with four smaller quadrants stacked underneath. He named his price, I countered at about a quarter of his price. He refused to bargain further. I offered him a third and he still refused. When told that that was my last price he became very restless and threatening. I thanked him and showed him the door but he refused to budge. My wife took our daughters to the bedroom while this stand-off continued for several minutes.

In the end I asked my wife to look out some old shirts from my wardrobe. She returned with three long sleeved white van Heusen shirts, each with collar and cuffs that were beginning to fray. When I offered these on top of my last price he took them grudgingly, rose and left.

Two weeks later I saw his photograph in the newspaper. He had been arrested for robbing a Shomolu barman of ten shillings at gun point. He was tried, found guilty and sentenced to death by firing squad on Bar Beach. It was widely believed that the ten bob robbery was a specimen charge and that the authorities had been looking for an excuse to top him for some time.

My wife was amused by one incident, though she told me that she was filled with apprehension at the time. Walking one afternoon on Bar Beach with our younger daughter and a friend, she was startled by the sudden arrival of three Hausas on horseback. One of them demanded to know what price she wanted for our daughter. Having been told that she was very definitely not for sale, he named his own price. Rebuffed again, he turned his attention to my wife's friend and offered half that price. Again denied, he galloped off with his colleagues. The friend was most offended at having been underpriced. My wife was offended at his total lack of interest in her.

One of my last tasks in Lagos was to respond to a tender calling for new telephone kiosks. A very tough specification it was too, necessarily, for if one thing was certain it was that the successful product would be put to uses its designers could never have contemplated. Our particular model had been carefully founded at Kirkintilloch in Scotland, with good back-up from toughened glass specialists on Merseyside. A similar model had successfully defied the ooyah-ooyah boys of Britain's toughest cities and would surely survive whatever Nigeria could throw at it. That proved to be the defining phrase.

All the bidders' representatives assembled at the Ministry's Falomo compound for the evaluation of the kiosks. There were samples from Japan, Belgium, France, Italy, Germany, Sweden and Britain. The evaluating officer appeared and immediately picked up an irregular shaped piece of concrete which he lobbed carefully from hand to hand as if to test its weight.

Without as much as a word of welcome he stepped to within three feet of the Japanese kiosk and hurled the concrete straight through one of its glass panels.

"Not strong enough," he barked as the little fellow from Yokohama, who had spent many weeks in meticulous planning before travelling half way round the globe, burst into a flurry of silent tears.

The Belgian offering looked well below specification and, as expected, presented minimal resistance. The French, Swedes and Italians fared little better, glass flying in all directions. They gazed in disbelief at each other, heads in their hands.

Before the evaluator could propel his missile at the German kiosk, its guardian, a large, heavily bewhiskered Bavarian, put up a show of resistance.

"Hey, you, come on," he started, waving his arms, "Zees ees not zee controlled test."

Smash!!!

In went the glass on Munich's finest.

The German rose to his full height , towering over the Nigerian and, scarlet with rage, screamed, "You see zees tree," pointing up into a huge kola, "You haf come down from higher zan ze highest branch of zees tree."

Now this is interesting, I thought. This is a pretty crude test but cannot compare with the assaults survived by similar kiosks back home. Ignoring the protests of our Bavarian friend, the wee fellow squared up to the British kiosk, hurled his concrete at point blank range and leapt into the air in agony as the projectile rebounded, struck him on the shin and clattered down onto his foot.

"Aaaagh!" he wailed, "Dat box is dangerous. It is disqualified. It has break my leg."

At least it gave our competitors something to cheer up about. We all rolled around in laughter.

"You deserve to veen," conceded the German, shaking my hand.

Heaven and the bank manager alone know how, but the contract was awarded to the Belgian apology for a vandal-proof kiosk. Perhaps it had qualities the rest of us had missed.

The day eventually arrived when we had to dispose of my

wife's car. It was advertised on the notice-board of the Ikoyi Club at a very reasonable Six Hundred pounds, exactly what I had paid the Michelin man for it. The advert was posted at lunchtime and, early the same evening, a friend from Ontario Hydro intercepted me with an offer, between matches at the tennis section.

"Would you like to try it out?" I asked.

"Well you came in it, so I assume it goes." he replied nonchalantly.

"OK, it's yours on one condition, that you give me a lift home."

The easiest deal of my life was concluded and I pocketed the cash.

Back at our apartment, later that evening, I answered a ring on the doorbell to be confronted by a Nigerian gentleman of beaming countenance who informed me that he had seen my advertisement and had arrived to purchase the car. I told him that the vehicle had already been sold, whereupon he insisted that negotiations had now been reopened.

"You will tell the other party that I am making a counter offer," he went on imperiously.

"I'm sorry, you must have misheard me," I interjected, "the deal has been concluded. The purchaser has the car and its documentation; I have accepted the payment."

He would not be moved and became increasingly indignant.

"I have promised this car to my wife and I certainly intend to keep that promise."

Stopping short of lecturing him in commercial law, I

invited him to seek whatever redress he thought fit elsewhere and closed the door. Threats of police action on the grounds of racial bias were being broadcast as he descended the staircase to his car below. Nothing further was heard from him, but I do hope his wife was not too disappointed.

After what seemed a decade, my tour of duty in Nigeria came to an end. We were a very relieved and much wiser family who boarded the KLM flight to Amsterdam than the one which had arrived in the autumn of 1972. At the same time there was a sense of sadness to be leaving behind a lot of good friends, both Nigerian and expatriate. Overseas opportunities were dwindling at that time. We had met families who had recently been squeezed out of Afghanistan, Iran, Tanzania and Zambia and felt that the era of expatriate residence for families could be coming to an end.

On arrival back in England we had to give our girls some time to readjust to the tempo of life and the change in culture.

That there might be problems had been apparent during our mid-tour leave when, on our first visit to an English supermarket, Louise, who was at that time five years old, had asked anxiously, "Mummy, why has that lady got African legs and a European head?"

No one wore tights in Nigeria! The girls made it and have been all the better for the experience.

I have revisited Lagos many times since but have never been able to recapture the spirit of the early seventies. The decline in economic fortune has scarred the nation badly and personal safety is much more at risk now than ever it was then. Even during the coups and attempted coups, there was never a real feeling of personal danger. The protagonists had their respective objectives and tended to leave the population at large alone to go about their daily business. As long as the command was strong, the armed forces remained reasonably disciplined. It has always been my opinion that Nigeria needs a strong, benign dictator rather than a Western style democracy. Many will disagree with me but I am sure that the Nigerian people would sooner have stability and fair shares for all than perpetual political bickering. I hope for their sakes that they get it.

Odabo, Oche.

Chapter 4
From New Delhi To Darjeeling

Having become firmly convinced that the rest of my life would be tied to Nigeria, people referring to me annoyingly and erroneously as "the Nigerian expert", it was a welcome surprise when I was asked to bone up on a proposal for an upgrade to the telephone system in Calcutta. I had never been to the sub-continent other than in transit and I welcomed the invitation to undertake contract negotiation there. This was to be the first of fifteen visits to India, one lasting only fifteen hours but usually for periods of three to six weeks.

Bursting into the New Delhi office of our Indian associate company at 9.00 a.m. on the first day of my first visit, I was put to seat and welcomed with a splendid pot of Assam's finest. After introductory courtesies, halfway through the morning that is, I was asked what I would like to do on my first day. Now, I had been UK based for the last couple of years, rehabilitated in the work ethic, de-tropicalised, de-humanised. I was a go-getter, had swallowed the Sales Manual propaganda hook, line and sinker.

"Well, before lunch I was hoping to see Mr. A, Mr. B and Mr. C. In the afternoon I was planning to see Mr. X, Mr. Y and Mr. Z."

There was a prolonged silence as a subdued Mr. Kohli sipped his tea.

Finally he looked up at me and mourned, "Sahib, I wish to live to be an *old* man," with a long drawn out *old*. "One meeting in the morning and one meeting in the afternoon is quite enough in the heat of India. I suggest that we go and discuss it over chai and cakes. I know the very place."

He clearly had no intention of setting up an itinerary on my terms, and he was absolutely right because no one else was going to hurry along at UK pace. To achieve any success I was going to have to readjust, so I did, much to the exasperation of my superiors back home. It was quite amusing in later years to see them fall in, one by one, with the Indian pace as they made their own forays to New Delhi.

My day to day guide was a splendid fellow named Ravi Shanker, not the famous one but with clear musical aspirations of his own. On several occasions as we walked from office to office to tea-shop to office around Connaught Place I would catch him singing to himself,
"From New Delhi to Darjeeling, I have always had this feeling - "

I am sure he saw me as some reincarnation of Peter Sellers whom, he assured me, all Indians adored.

India had not yet hosted the Asian Games and good hotels in New Delhi were few and far between. Not that there was much demand. The national motto at the time was "Be Indian - Buy Indian". Since the procurement of the tools for manufacture of the ubiquitous Morris Oxford automobile and Enfield motor cycle there had been a clamp down on foreign imports except in cases of dire national need, or, to put it more accurately, even in cases of dire national need. One met very few foreign businessmen in India in 1977.

My appointed abode was the palatial Ashoka Hotel, since renamed the Ashok. A government owned establishment, its clientele comprised mainly Indian public servants from other states, up to do business in the capital. PANAM included New Delhi on its round the world route, so we were subjected to the American blue rinse brigade on a regular basis. I say *we*! At times I was the only guest in this enormous sandstone edifice. I never saw it when there were more guests than staff. Occasionally, the peace was interrupted by large delegations of poker faced Russians who would take over whole wings, which were then cut off by security guards who made the Wigan front row look like choir boys. Crates of vodka helped form an impenetrable barricade, although I could never see why anyone would want to enter anyway. It may have been to stop Boris and Ivan escaping.

It was a bleak existence, hour after hour being spent on the crosswords in the Hindustan Times. A typical clue would be: *Our longest river.* Answer: *Severn.* Quite difficult when I had been weighing up the relative claims of various tributaries of the Ganges and Brahmaputra. The walk in a continuous circuit of the hotel, along the corridors, past the shops, behind the stage, past more shops and more corridors must have been going on for a mile in length. I did that circuit a hundred times. There were no appealing vegetables in the restaurant except spinach and I ate that until it was coming out of my ears. Oink, oink! There was no entertainment except one gnarled old pianist who rendered *ad nauseam* an approximation of *Misty* that Errol Garner would have been hard put to recognise.

Being the only guest in a five hundred room Indian hotel ensures attentive room service. The room wallahs are dependent on tips to supplement their meagre wages and the odds were stacked at two thousand to one against me. I rewarded the man who took me to my room, and the man who brought my luggage, and the man who brought me a bowl of fruit. Then I ran out of change, but still they kept coming. A man to turn back the bed sheets, a man with a vase of flowers, a man to check the lights, a man to check the plumbing, a man to collect my dhobi, a man with some more flowers, the stream was endless. I went out into the corridor and told the floor supervisor that I did not want any more room services that night. He professed to understand and stood leering at me with that fatuous look which told me that he too would be grateful for a few rupees.

On succeeding visits I worked out that if I could determine the key man on each shift and square him up in advance, it was not necessary to cough up for every attendance. Settling up and leaving had to be planned and executed with military precision if one was to avoid an emulation of the Pied Piper of Hamelin.

There were of course many other attractions in Delhi, but when you have visited them all four or five times you've had enough. I was in awe of the splendour of the Qutub Minar and the Delhi Fort. How long Lutyens must have pondered before he felt that his architectural plan for the modern New Delhi was worthy, I cannot imagine. I enjoyed the markets and bazaars, the craft shops and the parks, but always there was the loneliness of the Ashoka to return to.

Not to be missed were visits to the Taj Mahal at Agra and the Amber Palace at Jaipur. Both were comfortable (in one sense) return trips in one, albeit tiring, day, but well worth the effort. I visited the Taj three times over the years, always by coach and on each occasion wondering if this was to be the time when I would meet my Maker as we careered along narrow roads at breakneck speeds, rocking in and out of cattle, people and similar vehicles rattling along in the opposite direction.

The Agra trips also gave me the opportunity to visit Panch Mahal and Salim Chistie's Tomb at Fatehpur Sikri and Akbar's Tomb at Sikandra, all testimony to a history and culture which goes far beyond the concept of India as one big curry house.

You hear about the Taj Mahal and you see pictures of it but nothing can prepare you for the awe of being there, being surrounded by it, looking out over the Jumna River, the characteristic aromas on the breeze, sharing the experience with others. On my first visit, I gazed back from the Red Fort along the Jumna to the distant Taj, hazy and pink in the late afternoon light, and wondered whether I would ever see it again. Two minutes later, sitting on a marble slab, high up on the fort, I was informed by our guide that anyone who sits on that slab is destined to return. And so it came to pass.

On one visit to New Delhi I was reunited at the British High Commission with an Edinburgh friend from Nigeria days. As we were enjoying a leisurely knock on the BHC tennis courts, he asked me whether I had ever refereed a soccer match. As it happened, I had taken charge of several during my army days in Germany. That included one epic encounter between the Royal Military Police and the Royal Air Force Police, Monkeys versus Snowdrops, in which I had ordered off two from each side and confined myself to my billet for the next two weeks. He averred that I was suitably qualified and cajoled me into reffing a match on the following Saturday between a Diplomatic Enclave Select XI and a college team from the city.

The diplomats were a formidable bunch. My friend had been on the books of Heart of Midlothian and played for Tynecastle Athletic until he sacrificed his footballing career in favour of the Foreign Office. A tall, blonde, muscular fellow with Feyenoord connections looked pretty useful, as did a mountain of a Swedish centre forward. The rest of the team were pretty fit and were clearly not going to be anybody's pushover.

When I saw the opposition players, I winced. They were all from Himachal Pradesh with an average height of five feet plus a whisker and all took the field in bare feet. The pitch was one of dozens in a huge, unfenced recreational expanse near the University. The grass was sparse. The crowd, which seemed to accrue from nowhere, would have done an English second division match proud.

As soon as they kicked off it was clear that the Indian lads were on a hiding to nothing. They were five nil down within ten minutes. The word went round among some of the diplomats to ease off and just play possession football. Easing off is not easy when you are so superior and some of your numbers do not understand the phrase. By half-time they had banged in thirteen without reply.

The heat was obviously going to assist the Indians and, sure enough, the diplomats began to wilt in the second half. Still, another three headers had found the net (how can a five feet zero centre half legitimately challenge a six feet five striker?) when I decided to ameliorate the spectators and so avoid any end-of-match unpleasantness.

Taking my cue from a crunching Norwegian tackle on the halfway line, I awarded a free kick to Himachal. As the ball came back off the head of the Dutchman, I blew again.

"Climbing!" I called.

"I am already one metre higher than him. How can I be climbing?" was the startled reaction.

Asserting my authority I sent the defensive wall back ten yards into the penalty area. Boof! A teak tough Himalayan foot sent the ball cannoning into the chest of my Scottish friend.

Toot!

"Penalty!" I announced.

"Och! Come away Ref, the ball hit my chest."

I was resolute.

"I'm in charge and I say it caught your forearm."

You would have thought it was the Edinburgh derby.

"For heaven's sake Ref, it was never a penalty."

He could hardly contain himself when I rebuked, "One more word out of you and you're off."

Then, under my breath, I muttered to him, "Come on man, you're sixteen up. Give them a consolation goal for crying out aloud. They'll go home happy."

"But it wisnae a penalty," he went on as if his whole career had been besmirched.

The Australian goalkeeper had read the script and flew spectacularly in the opposite direction to the ball. The crowd erupted. The Himachal players danced and cartwheeled. The cheering must have been audible in the Chandni Chowk. They did not give a toss about losing another three goals; they had scored in an international match. After the final whistle there were handshakes and smiles all round as we made for the showers.

I was really enjoying the cool refreshing cascade when a plaintive voice came from the next cubicle, "That was never a penalty, the Ref needs his eyes tested."

It was only at the bar in the Australian High Commission after the coach drive back that I conceded that it wasn't a penalty and explained why it had been given.

"I thought you were the diplomat," I chided him.

Fitba' is serious stuff in Scotland!

I had one other encounter with football in New Delhi. An international telecommunications exhibition had been arranged at which I was to be the Company's sole UK representative. Manning our modest equipment stand, I was underwhelmed by the number of visitors when, an hour into the first morning, I glanced to my left and saw my Hungarian neighbour obviously having similar thoughts. I nodded to him and he nodded back.

I bade him "Good morning!" but he shrugged and struggled out, "No English."

We smiled and resumed our solemn postures.

A few minutes later I looked at him and called, "Ferenc

Puskas."

His face lit up as he responded, "Bobby Charlton."

On we went through, Hidegkuti, Banks, Buzansky, Stiles, Lantos, Hurst, Czibor, Peters, Sandor, Ball, Fenyevesi, Cohen, Koscis, Moore, and the rest. He knew the whole of the England World Cup winning team and I could recall most of the Magical Magyars from the Fifties. The ice was broken. Somehow we managed to convey meaning to each other and, after his sampling of my whisky and my tasting of his vodka, we left for a very cordial, if stilted, lunch at the Oberoi. Every exchange brought a handshake and smile.

"Manchester United!"

"Honved!"

"Prosit!"

A real bonus came my way one Saturday morning when I was asked in our Delhi office what my interests were away from work. I mentioned a lifelong interest in railways and made reference to the splendid array of steam traction that I had observed on the way in from the airport.

"Ah, that is the National Railway Museum," I was told, "you should visit it."

Without further ado, Mr. Fixit had lifted the phone and was soon speaking to a senior railway official at Delhi Locomotive Works.

"Malhotra, Sahib, Kumar here. I have a visitor with me from Rugby in England . Oh, you were trained by LMS at Rugby. Very good, Sahib. Yes, we can be there in one hour. Thank you, Sahib, a pleasure."

I had visited Derby Works in my childhood and had

stood next to the London Midland Scottish's largest, the Beyer-Garret articulated locos, but nothing had prepared me for the enormous scale of some of these North Indian giants. Even more thrilling, they were still operational, soft bursts of steam belying the colossal power within. Out in the cleaning yard were two engines which had completed their work for the day and were having their fireboxes cleaned out, and there on the tracks beneath the mass of metal were two groups of parlous looking women, scavenging amongst the discarded clinker and smouldering ashes for any fuel that could be salvaged. What an existence!

India is a nation of huge contrasts, from the richest of the rich to the poorest of the poor. The former is a slender pinnacle, the latter is a very broad base. The yawning gulf in technology between the caesium clock which looked down on me on my first visit to the Telecommunications Research Centre in New Delhi and the clapped out clackety-clack telephone exchanges upon which the sub-continent depended was a reflection of the disparity in the spread of the nation's wealth. Although the vast fortunes of the maharajahs had been substantially neutralised, there still remained concentrations of huge private resources, anomalistic against the backdrop of national poverty. But whereas the atomic clock was a key support in the quest for Indian solutions to Indian problems, the entrepreneurial investment and creativity of the private sector was stifled by the bureaucracy and red tape of successive governments to such an extent that technological capability and achievement ran completely out of kilter.

To anyone from a developed country not familiar with the poverty which is encountered daily on the streets of towns and cities in the developing world, the initial impact is one of shock and revulsion. This in the course of time turns to sympathy and a sense of helplessness. Most become inured to it and carry on as if it did not exist. Walking through the Chowranghee, the busiest shopping centre in Calcutta, one would inevitably be pursued by beggars. Give them anything and they would be replaced by ten thousand more. It was better to avoid eye contact with these hapless individuals. Unless one had the time and dedication of a Mother Theresa, there was little one could do to help them. At least the clinker sifters at Delhi Loco Works had a purpose and a task to perform. In that respect they were the lucky ones. It's all relative.

One lesson you do need to learn is never to mock the humble. Together with two technical colleagues I had accompanied a large tender document from London to New Delhi. It was well packed and sealed but, as often happens, certain amendments were necessary before it could finally be submitted. Time was at a premium, since the submission deadline was later the same morning.

Having cleared airport customs the first task was to obtain transport. None of the taxi drivers felt able to cope with fifteen volumes of tender documents, ten copies of each, until up popped a cheery Sikh with a roof rack on his cab. Some cartons went in the boot, the lid of which remained open, some went aloft, doubling the height of the vehicle, while we three passengers hunched inside with our suitcases on our knees.

You have never seen a Morris Oxford under such duress. It crawled along the highway, groaned it's way round bends, occupants leaning over to compensate the centrifugal motion, but it got us to Connaught Place. That is what mattered to us and that is what mattered to our Sikh conductor, regardless of any possible damage to his suspension. He received a London scale fare and deserved every rupee.

Amendments duly carried out, we urgently needed new transport to ferry us to Ministry Headquarters. The office cars, which we had banked on, were not available. One had gone to Haridwar for an accounts audit, the other had gone *kaput*. New Delhi was at its busiest with not a taxi to be had. We asked about hiring a van but had no joy there. A truck perhaps? Not for several hours. Then I spotted a downtrodden old chappie in a turban and loin cloth accompanying an empty relic of a cart drawn by an emaciated donkey.

Grabbing Mr. Shanker, who would be needed as interpreter, I raced down the stairs, out into Connaught Place and hailed the bemused cart wallah. The whole of India seemed to be watching as three Englishmen and an Indian businessman, dressed in their city finery, accompanied this improbable load on a cart which smelled almost as bad as its owner, through the streets of the capital and through the wrought iron gates of the Ministry, much to the consternation of the Ministry guards, I might add. The deadline was met. The cart wallah went on his way with the equivalent of a year's earnings and a fine story to tell.

I made one of the biggest gaffs of my career at the Ministry in Delhi. My protagonist at the contract negotiation was a very astute Sikh gentleman who welcomed me with great courtesy and respect. We rattled along through the terms and conditions at a healthy pace until we became bogged down over a clause which would have allowed the customer to offset claims against our parent company or any of its subsidiaries against sums due to our section of the company. I could not accept his wording and he claimed that it was enshrined in law. By way of concession he pledged that, although the condition must exist, he would never apply it.

Recalling a particular commercial training session back in England and the words of our tutor at that time, I naively uttered, "But Sir, you may not be sitting behind that desk tomorrow."

Wow! He exploded.

I recall his flashing eyes glowering through gold rimmed spectacles below a scarlet turban as he rose, stretched himself to his full height and thundered, "You are dealing with the Government of India, not some tin-pot banana republic in Africa!"

The situation was only recovered when he was sure that I had taken his grievance on board. Three days later I turned up a case precedent in a legal tome and the clause was deleted.

Friends often ask me whether I like India and I always counter by asking them to which particular part of India they are referring. It is a country of so many contrasts, stretching from the Himalayan snows in the North to the near-equatorial South, with the arid Rajasthan Desert on one side and the tea plantations and forests of Assam on the other. I like, for different reasons, all of those parts which I have visited but there is so much that I have still to see.

Calcutta, with its quaintly named Dum Dum Airport, is on the surface a dirty, over-congested squalid looking city. Examined more closely it is a city rich in culture, with fine people and some beautiful and majestic buildings.

I had been told in the Delhi office that I would find plenty of Banerjee, Mukerjee and Chatterjee in Calcutta, but definitely no Enerjee. What a travesty! The place was abounding with energy, men running with heavily laden carts, others driving cycle taxis, people scuttling hither and thither in all directions. It was like a human ant-hill.

Having enjoyed the railway atmosphere at Delhi, it was fascinating to obtain the perspective from the Bengal end of the line at Howrah Station. The non-stop bustle, the toing and froing of people with their loads, the constant cacophony of voices and station announcements, the smoke laden atmosphere, the sheer vitality of the place took me back to a different age.

Spending a day visiting temples and museums would not have been part of my itinerary but for the intervention of colleagues at our Indian company's Calcutta headquarters. What a treat I would have missed. The Jain, Kali and Dakshineshwar temples, the Buddhist Pagoda, the Belur Math, and the Victoria Memorial are creations worthy of any great city. I spent hours in the museum of the Victoria Memorial and learned more about Anglo-Indian history on that day than in my entire life before or after.

One sturdy character at Calcutta HQ had recently returned from an ascent of Dhaulagiri and had fascinating tales to tell of that and a previous ascent of Annapurna. I had gazed in awe at both from an internal Indian Airways flight. To sit and listen to someone who had actually been on them was music to my ears.

My favourite city in India has to be Bangalore. Sitting high on a plateau in the southern state of Karnataka, it has a beautiful warm, dry climate. It is easy to see why it is called the tree city of India. The streets are wide and tree lined, the building line is low. Everywhere the nostrils are soothed by the fragrant scent of sandalwood. There is that wonderful, mellow feeling that time is plentiful and pressure is a million miles away. The Churchill Memorial Hospital indicates the strong historic links with Britain and everywhere I went I was made very welcome.

I was standing at the reception counter in the Bangalore Ashoka one afternoon, having just flown in from Madras, when my attention was caught by the reflection in the mirror opposite of the gentleman next to me. He immediately appeared familiar to me and yet, I thought, I know no one in this part of India and there must be thousands of moustachioed Indian men who look just like him. I looked again and it registered.

"You'll not find a wicket like Edgbaston here," I dropped out casually.

He looked into the mirror, then turned to me, smiled and asked "Are you from Warwickshire?"

I confirmed that I lived in Rugby and introduced myself.

Alvin Kallicharran needed no introduction.

"Come over and meet the boys," he breezed.

I had had no idea that the West Indies cricket team were in town for a test match against India so it came as a big surprise. A formidable group they were too!

It was late in the year and, learning that I would be returning home within a few days, they all set to and wrote their Christmas cards and letters for me to post back in England, where several of the West Indians had set up home anyway. A small delegation of British Members of Parliament who were relaxing in a corner of the lounge soon locked on to what was happening and added their own correspondence to the rapidly growing pile of mail.

Vivid memories flood back, when I think of Bangalore, of an outing to the Nandi Hills. On the slopes of the foothills an army of young women was busily picking tea leaves. On the return journey, under the setting sun, the road below was a blaze of colour as these same girls made their way home, their baskets on their heads. A myriad saris in the brightest of gold, pink, turquoise, emerald, scarlet, sapphire and orange, gliding along, absolutely erect as if floating on air.

Higher up in the Nandi Hills was the one spot on earth where I have felt most out of place. The source of the Andhra Ganga is a site of pilgrimage, the greenish blue holy waters reached by descending a square shaped basin, flanked on all sides by three hundred or so steps. Midst the devotion of the many visitors, I felt extremely awkward, as if I was intruding in a place where I had no right to be. Close by was the spot where Mr. Nehru had his summer retreat. It was not difficult to understand why he had chosen this beautiful part of his vast country. It was serenity itself.

I learned something about Indian welfare while in a meeting with a director of a large Bangalore manufacturing company. As we chatted in his opulent mahogany panelled office, he invited me to smoke, a habit to which he was not himself addicted. As I took a cigarette from my case, he rang a small handbell which he had taken from a drawer in his desk. In stepped an elderly worker, shuffled over to the desk, withdrew an ornate cigarette lighter and held it aloft for me to light my cigarette. Mission completed he replaced the lighter, bowed and shuffled backwards out of the room. I looked on, bemused by this little cameo.

"You are thinking that it would have been just as easy for me to operate the lighter as it was to ring the bell," said the director, correctly as it happened.

"That gentleman also has a family to support and the few rupees that I pay him serves the same purpose as the National Assistance in your country. That is one of the misjudgements you make when you talk of Indian overmanning."

The two punkah wallahs out on the veranda continued to draw lazily on the cords of the fans. An aged stenographer in an adjacent office tapped out a discordant *andantino* on an antique typewriter. Since that day I have viewed Indian industrial on-costing in a different light.

Most visitors to India do not see beyond the major cities and that is a great pity. It is when you venture out into the villages that you sense the real pulse of the country.

Contrary to the popular concept in the West, the Indians in India are a very serene people, proud in their bearing and demeanour and yet humble in their personal esteem. A culture developed and honed over thousands of years has developed standards which are respected and maintained without question by the vast majority.

The burgeoning corruption which one meets at the higher commercial levels is alien to the national psyche and is all the more regrettable. When I first visited the country in 1977 I found little compared with that to be found in the Middle East, Africa and South America at that time. Twenty years later and the upper echelons were right there alongside the leaders.

My urge to venture off the beaten track had developed down in Karnataka when I wondered what sort of life the tea pickers went back to after their hours of toil on the hillsides. Eventually I got my wish and, as unobtrusively as I could, accompanied my host through a totally unsuspecting village in the vicinity of Mysore.

The experience was akin to a journey back in time. Bullocks strained as they hauled their rickety carts loaded high with wood, fruit and all manner of provisions essential to the local community. Children splashed around a water pump, their main purpose being to collect water but delighting in the opportunity to splash their hot little bodies. Women cooked and laundered while men toiled under the unrelenting sun. Animals and poultry contested stray morsels beside the freshly swept paths. There was a vitality about the place and yet at the same time a relaxed self containment. Politics and materialism seemed quite remote, although I do not doubt that there was plenty of the former lurking behind the peaceful facade.

It was interesting to observe the two features which I have mentioned, the bullock cart and the village water pump. While in New Delhi, killing the hours at the Ashoka Hotel, I had read in a national newspaper about a postgraduate assignment undertaken by one of the seats of higher learning. I believe it was Bombay University who set up a project to improve the quality of rural life. Two of the specifics to be studied were the bullock cart and the village pump. I was fascinated to learn that after several weeks of endeavour it was decided that in neither case could any substantial improvement be achieved. Of course one could design far superior carts and motor driven pumps were available at the leading edge of technology. The key factor however was that the students were constrained to the same resources and economical deprivations which governed the lives of the villagers. The old bullock cart, with wheels which wobbled at every rut and mound, had been developed over centuries and wobbled with a purpose, to compensate for the rough ground on which it was required to travel. In fact the University decided that, within the parameters allowed, it was a perfect design.

A similar conclusion was applied to the water pump. Bearings had been tried and small motors. But these went faulty and replacement parts were either too expensive or not locally available, usually both. I found it all to be most illuminating.

In one instance I stood for some time absolutely

fascinated, watching a gentleman of considerable age, engaged in the manual stringing of squash and badminton racquets. There was not a machine in sight. However he had the biggest, sturdiest hallux I have ever been privileged to see. Holding the racquet frame between his feet and deftly threading the gut with his fingers, the critical operation was the fine tensioning which was gauged with great precision by his remarkable right big toe. The mind boggles at the effect on human evolution of generations of big toes put to such purpose! Perhaps I was witnessing just that.

I rest contented that I have seen a little, albeit very little, of some of the multifarious sides of India. It is a fascinating kaleidoscope of nature and humanity. Strangely, the music of a Russian seaman, Nikolay Andreyevich Rimsky-Korsokov, illustrates the atmosphere of space and serenity of that vast country in his *Song Of India*, but it is the traditional Indian music, especially the classical Hindustani *sarangi* which captures the true essence of India. Should you have the opportunity to visit this enchanting land, my advice is to leave behind your Western mantle and let the mysticism of *Bharat* wash over you.

Chapter 5
Back to Africa

In spite of my heavy involvement with India, I had continued to retain an interest in Africa and it was a moment of joyful anticipation when I was appointed to oversee the company's marketing interests throughout Africa. The only exceptions to this were Egypt, which we included in the Middle East, and South Africa, the management of which was incompatible with that of its neighbours. I was told by my Managing Director at the outset that every day spent in the United Kingdom would be a day wasted. Well, not everyday because there was an abundance of preparation and debriefing to go through, including meetings in London at the Department of Trade and Industry and at the various embassies and trade missions. But Africa was my oyster and I set about it with relish.

My predecessor had operated out of Nairobi, but I preferred Harare as a base. By that time the country had settled down as Zimbabwe. Southern Rhodesia and Salisbury were but sentimental memories and I was cheered by the will of the people to pull in the same direction and get along together. For better or for worse independence had been broadly accepted. There were pockets of resentment which surfaced from time to time but these appeared to be in a small minority.

I came across one office in Bulawayo where the man in charge was a white South African who claimed to have killed many of these black people when he was in the

Rhodesian Army and would willingly kill many more if asked to do so in the future.

When I mentioned my surprise at his being able to get away with employing so few blacks in Mr. Mugabe's Zimbabwe, the response was, "They have not been in touch with the human race long enough."

Meikle's Hotel in Harare was one of those jewels that would add to the stature of any city in the world. There was an air of gentility about the place that set it apart from the plastic and chrome of the modern day pretenders. My Middle East counterpart had spent some time in these parts as a major in the Royal Signals. He had asked me to look up a few of his old chums and pay them his regards. One of these was a very senior officer in the Zimbabwe Armed Forces. I had telephoned him and introduced myself and my mission. With great enthusiasm he offered to meet me in the foyer lounge at Meikles, from where we would go to dinner. Quite innocently I asked the lobby manager if he would be kind enough to tip me the wink when the officer arrived.

"Oh! My God!" he exclaimed. "Is he coming here?"

What had I triggered off?

"You will not need to be told when he arrives," the poor fellow went on, "it will be self-evident."

What did he mean? I had once witnessed the crashing entry of Joshua Nkomo into the foyer of the Strand Palace Hotel in London and so was aware of the startling impact of which Zimbabweans were capable.

I sure found out in the fullness of time. In through the revolving door burst this huge figure in Army uniform, covered in scrambled egg and other insignia of high rank, and beaming from ear to ear. As he entered the foyer everyone else fell back in awe. I had no difficulty in identifying my man. I strode up to him and offered my hand. After all but dislocating my shoulder he asked after the health of our mutual friend. At that point the lobby manager stepped up, asked if there was any service he could provide and immediately wished he hadn't.

"Please leave us alone, we have much to talk about," said my companion, brushing him away as one does a troublesome mosquito.

We dined well that evening. If I had been with the President himself we could not have received better service.

Being a relatively tall person at 1.93 metres, I am momentarily thrown when confronted by someone taller than myself, particularly if that person is a woman. This experience had befallen me quite dramatically in 1960 on Princes Street in Edinburgh. While awaiting the arrival of a friend I suddenly found myself surrounded by a throng of the tallest ladies I had ever seen or imagined existed. Turning round to determine whence they came, I spotted the plaque on the door of *The Tall Women's Society of Great Britain*.

This experience was to recur on the outskirts of Harare when I visited the film set where they were shooting *King Solomon's Mines*. Again I had not been expecting it when I was confronted by an army of the most stunning female giants imaginable. What a pesky little mortal I felt before these veritable goddesses. Where they disappeared to for the rest of the time is a mystery to me. More's the pity!

As with all developing nations in Africa there was business to be had in Zimbabwe, if you went with a bucketful of aid. We were British and the British tax payer will be gratified to know that his hard earned taxes were parted with very sparingly indeed. This did not assist my cause at all. I was losing out to the Japanese, Swedes, French and others who, unlike the UK Government, regarded telecommunications as basic infrastructure. Hospitals, roads, agriculture, schools, yes, but could I convince anyone in London of the basic need for good communications? No chance.

There was one ardent soul in London who listened with great sympathy to the sad entreaties of a government minister from Tanzania.

"Yes," he encouraged, "there must be something we can do."

Before you could say "Tanganyika" two of us were on a flight to Dar-es-Salaam to assist in the planning of a new telephone network linking all provincial capitals with each other and with Dar.

After three days of quiet industry, we presented our initial draft and were promptly told to be in our hotel lobby with our baggage and passports at 8.00 a.m. the following morning, ready to go to the airport. Our initial reaction was that we had offended and were about to be tossed out of the country.

Not a bit of it. We were whisked in a small jet up to Kilimanjaro Airport. What a delightful modern anachronism that was after the jaded, clapped out facilities we had just left at Dar. A safari wagon was waiting and we were taken past the magnificent snow-capped Mount Kilimanjaro and Mount Meru into Arusha for a pleasant lunch before the long drive up into the North West Highlands, where we were installed in the Ngorongoro Crater Lodge.

The reason behind this unexpected adventure was to give the technical boffins in the Ministry time to digest and comment on the plans which we had drawn up. Usually I look forward to my first visit to a country but, such was the bad publicity surrounding the tough politics of Tanzania, that I had been very wary of this visit. Now here we were, standing on the edge of one of nature's most beautiful creations, a fifteen miles diameter caldera surrounded by two thousand feet high walls. Down in the basin were twenty -five thousand wild animals including almost everything that Africa has to offer. We were told that giraffes, of which we had seen several on the drive past Lake Manyara, were not to be found in the crater in the absence of acacia trees but that did not dampen our enthusiasm one little bit. This was like visiting the zoo big time.

Sitting on the equator that evening, by a roaring log fire, we asked ourselves what we had done to deserve such treatment - or what we were expected to give in return.

Rising early the following morning I opened the door of my chalet to be confronted by a massive variant of the ox, a bull according to its undercarriage, which did not seem in any particular hurry to leave. I had not been briefed on the temperament of this particular species, but I knew it was wild and was not prepared to take any chances, so I sat and watched it for half an hour through the window before I was sure that it was no longer in my line of approach to the lodge's central complex. Cows in an English meadow give me the willies; this feral hulk was in a different league altogether.

Another surprise confronted us as we descended into the crater. There below us lay a pride of twenty plus lions, lazing on the grass after what appeared to have been a successful night's hunting. Bisecting them was a small procession of domestic cattle being driven casually along by a Masai herdsman who looked as if he was taking a stroll through Hyde Park. All this was new to me. I had hitherto believed that lions are ferocious beasts which kill anything within range without the slightest compunction. One lives and learns.

At a far remote spot we stopped by a small reed shrouded pool to quaff the packed lunches with which we had been provided. As I peered into the water on the off chance of seeing yet another exotic creature, our guide called to me, not with any urgency, to watch out for crocodiles which may be lurking in the reeds.

I jumped ten feet high and ten feet backwards at the mere thought of becoming a crocodile's lunch. My compatriot meantime held up a sandwich to undertake a closer inspection of its contents. He need not have bothered as a kite with no such fads swept down, grazing his forehead with its knife-like wings, and relieved him of it.

Fauna in zoos are one thing; big cats, reptiles and raptors in the wild are quite another. Never having been entirely at ease with the possible presence of adders on Goat Fell, mountain goats on Ben A'an or wild cats on Mount Keen, I certainly was not in the running for bravery awards in this predators' parlour and disappeared hot foot into the back of the safari wagon to consume the remainder of my lunch.

On our return to Dar-es-Salaam we learned that the Tanzanian marathon champion, who was a strongly fancied contender for Olympic gold, had been shot dead while out training by soldiers who thought that, because he was running , he must be a criminal making his escape.

My next visit to Dar-es-Salaam saw me installed in the once grand Kilimanjaro Hotel. I was one of three guests, along with a Russian lady who spent every daylight hour by the hotel swimming pool and whose presence was never explained, and a German whom I was compelled to meet at dinner in the vast empty restaurant.

Already well into my second course, I espied the Teutonic visitor speaking to the head waiter at the door. Having taken his bearings he marched towards my table with the directness of an iron filing to a magnet. Click went the heels as he stopped and stood stiffly to attention.

"Good eefening, I am Decker, za expert on Economics from Shermany."

Thanks for letting me know pal, I'll make sure we don't raise that as a topic of conversation.

"How nice, how can I help you Herr Decker?"

"I haf decided to dine viz you."

I never did determine whether he was from the Peoples' Republic or the Federal Republic, probably the former, seeing where we were. In fact I hardly got a word in edgeways. It was as if he had been incarcerated for several years with no one to listen to his endless drone. For two hours I heard but I did not listen.

Dar-es-Salaam was at that time suffering daily power outages. Unlike its East African neighbours, the capital is on the coast and therefore suffers the same clinging humidity as Maputo and Mombasa. The Ministry building was occupied in hierarchical order with the most senior at the top, coming down through the ranks to the peons at the bottom. The power outages did not help my cause. On one day I had to ascend three times from ground level to the twenty-third floor, questioning at every step why they did not invert the pecking order. Security, I guess. Still, it is one way to keep fit.

The purpose of my second visit was to inform the Minister that the network expansion project had fallen through as there was no aid forthcoming from London. The gentleman who had intimated that there would be had, I was informed, spoken without authority. I had been dreading this moment. For days leading up to the visit I had pondered over the wisdom of meeting the Minister personally to convey the bad news.

Tanzania was at the time an unpredictable political entity and the United Kingdom was not its number one ally. After listening to my apology, the Minister leaned back, high in his chair, scrutinising me carefully. The dreaded tirade never materialised.

"Do you know," he said quietly, "I never expected there to be any aid. I will say that I do admire your courage in coming here to tell me to my face. It would have been quite easy for you to have sent me a letter or a telex from London. The fact that you took the trouble and the time to come to my office and told me personally is worthy of my respect. Thank you for trying."

I have not had occasion to return to Tanzania again. I felt as I left that I was leaving a very friendly people who had been condemned by their politicians to spend many more years in the economic doldrums. All the revenues generated by their utilities were being hauled in by the exchequer to supplement the military budget, to fight whom no one was quite sure, resulting in no capital reinvestment and inevitable decay of the existing infrastructure. Consequently the donor nations had all turned their backs leaving a vicious downward spiral. What a sad demise for a country with so much potential.

The nation on which Dame Fortune was beginning to smile at that time was Uganda, which I visited with two of my colleagues shortly after the departure of Idi Amin. The country was just beginning to open up again to foreigners and access was somewhat diverse. The Israelis had recently shot up Entebbe Airport and tensions were still uncomfortably high.

We took a Sabena flight from Brussels which proceeded in an ever decreasing circle, calling at Kigali in Rwanda and Bujumbura in Burundi before finally delivering us to Entebbe. Memories of my childhood philately returned: Ruanda-Urundi, filed under 'B' as a Belgian Trust Territory! Little things like that titillate the imagination.

An old friend had related to me the experiences of a motor-cycle expedition which he had accomplished from

Cairo to the Cape of Good Hope, in the days when the road was in good condition and colonial control allowed such an undertaking. I remember him telling me that Uganda, with its Mountains of the Moon, was the most beautiful of all the countries he had passed through, and the friendliest. It was difficult to reconcile such friendliness with the atrocities that those same people had perpetrated on each other so recently.

This was in my mind as we left Entebbe for the short drive to Kampala. These were early days. Tension was still high and remnants of rebel activity still continued. We had only driven three miles when we ran up to a road block. Whether friend or foe I had no idea.

"Do as they say," was the concise advice of our driver.

We stepped down from the car and immediately found ourselves peering down the business end of Kalashnikovs being held by kids no older than thirteen or fourteen. They demanded to know who we were and why we were in Uganda.

When the questioning ceased and they started chatting to each other, I asked my immediate protagonist whether he could write.

"What you mean?" he asked.

"Can you write your name?" I continued.

"Why you ask dat?"

"Because I have gift for you."

"What is dis gift?"

"It is a pen, a very special pen. If you will point that thing somewhere else I will show it to you. It is in my pocket," I said patting my chest with my raised elbow.

"You will show it to me," he instructed, laying his rifle on the deck.

As he did so, I produced the biggest biro pen you have ever seen, an advertising hand-out from a company back in Nottingham.

"You see," I said, "it writes. It is for you."

He took it and scribbled delightedly on the palm of his hand, just as I had done.

"Do you have brothers?" was the next natural question, judging by the anticipation and curiosity on the faces of his buddies.

"Yes I have brothers."

Out from my pocket I took another two similar pens and handed them to him. Now he had power over the other two.

"Thank you, Sir, you are my brother, you may go."

I still had another three pens in my other inside pocket but fortunately did not need them on the remainder of the road to Kampala.

Kampala was full of contradictions. The hotels had not yet recovered from the troubles, nor had their restaurants and yet we found a superb little eatery on the road up to the city water tank where a Ugandan lady, newly returned from exile in Paris, served us with the most succulent of steaks in some exotic sauce.

The streets were seemingly safe during the day but after curfew they turned into a shooting gallery, bullets whining and ricocheting throughout the night. We were told that there was no actual trouble but the guards had become so conditioned to night attacks that they took a pot at anything that moved, a cat or dog or even perhaps the shadow of a waving tree. It was a relief when dawn arrived and normality returned.

The people were extremely friendly, as my old friend had said, and were pleased that we actually wanted to do business with them. When I phoned the Minister to make an appointment he told me to stay put and came round to our hotel to hold the meeting, insisting on buying the first round of drinks himself. I had not come across that before in Africa or anywhere else.

Another unique performance was that of the local harlots. Excited at finding new meat in town they were buzzing around the Imperial Hotel like flies. Undeterred by our constant refusal to avail of their pleasures, they hung around, dropping the asking price every hour on the hour until 10.00 p.m. when they offered themselves free of charge.

The barman smiled and confided, "It is too dangerous for them to venture out into the street now. They just want a free bed for the night."

Next morning, when we came down to breakfast, they were all still there, curled up and snoring on the settees in the hotel lounge. The carpet beneath them was inches deep in huge, translucent-winged crickets which the porter was busily sweeping into the street. The girls were oblivious to it all.

The final surprise was the offer, by the Minister, of transport to Entebbe in the limousine of the newly appointed Ugandan High Commissioner to the United Kingdom, who was catching the same flight to Nairobi *en route* to London.

"His Excellency has enemies too," we were warned, "but he also has powerful friends."

As we drove out past the war ravaged Lake Victoria Hotel, diplomatic pennant fluttering on the bonnet, a convoy of outriders ensured the security of my remaining biros. The red carpet treatment which we received at Entebbe Airport was most unexpected and greatly appreciated.

Our departure was somewhat less frenzied than that of the British Caledonian flight which had scraped off the ground at the onset of the Amin era, loaded to the gunwales with desperate people whose baggage included everything but the kitchen sink. Both the B-Cal station manager and the air traffic controller had turned their backs until the roar of the jets told them that it was safely airborne.

Nairobi was something of an anticlimax after the unpredictability of Uganda. All the expected Hooray Henries were there at the bar of the Norfolk Hotel, knocking them back in the late afternoon and putting the world to rights. One who stood out from an otherwise amorphous crowd was a very odd young German who spoke excellent English, but always in rhyming couplets. Not quite Goethe, in fact nothing like Goethe,

he found the British very strange
and tried to keep them out of range.

An hour in his company was akin to reading a Rupert book. Amazingly, subjects of considerable gravity were given the same poetic treatment and with great fluidity.

It is one of my regrets that I never managed to get out of Nairobi to visit the much vaunted delights of Amboseli and the Masai Mara. Someone had constructed a mini game park on the outskirts so I had to make do with that. However, the white capped cone of Kilimanjaro to the South constantly reminded me that I was in Kenya and not at Knowsley Safari Park.

Unfortunately for me, the company had a strong local sales and manufacturing unit in Nairobi which rendered my efforts somewhat redundant. There were too many delicately poised commercial relationships to be put at risk by an occasional interloper. My visits were essentially transitory and of short duration.

Most of my regional travels during the Eighties took me through Harare Airport, from where it was a short hop to Zambia, Botswana , Malawi or Swaziland.

After the comparative affluence of Zimbabwe, Zambia provided a strong reminder that African nations had not made equal progress since gaining their independence. Whereas the shops in Harare were well stocked, the streets were busy, and businesses were thriving, Lusaka and Ndola appeared very short on resource and progress.

Danger lurked in the shape of uniformed authority, always on the look out for a fast buck. The junction where the Ndola road meets the road from Kitwe to Lusaka was a notorious spot for muggings and had to be approached with great caution.

It was between Ndola and Lusaka that I had my second sighting of the Chinese funded Tanzam railway. The architectural magnificence of the Dar-es-Salaam terminus had heralded great engineering exploits ahead. Here in Zambia the line looked much less flamboyant, floundering in the desolation of a bereft economy. The railway headquarters at Kabwe portrayed a more realistic state of affairs. Once proud old steam locomotives now appeared both comical and forlorn with vegetation sprouting from every orifice, some of the offending bushes having reached comparative maturity.

Please do not get the idea that the railways of central Africa are totally defunct. As an illustration of their competence and integrity, I witnessed the arrival at Ndola of a package containing electrical spare parts which had been shipped from England twelve years previously. Originally landed at Lobito in Angola, the package, measuring about eight cubic feet, had been despatched on the Benguela Railway to Ndola in Zambia via Lubumbashi in Zaire. Caught up in the Angolan civil war, it had been stranded in an up-country sidings until a cessation of hostilities, whereupon it had been recovered and sent back down to Benguela. From Angola it was shipped to Durban in South Africa and routed by rail up through Botswana and Zimbabwe and into Zambia at Victoria Falls. Goods and documentation were all in pristine condition on arrival. I wondered whether the insurance claim had been settled with such expedition.

The run-down lot of the average Zambian was in marked contrast to the flashy opulence on view at the Ndola Club. Big spending, immaculately suited city types lolled around, their black Mercedes-Benz limousines flooding the car park as if presenting a fingers up to their less fortunate fellow countrymen. Arrange an international convention, budget for the best and share the spoils afterwards was a preferred short cut to comfortable living.

Botswana was a tremendous contrast to both Zambia and Zimbabwe. Gaborone, the capital, has a tiny population, 133,000, compared with Harare's 1.3 million and it is difficult to appreciate that this laid back overgrown village is the capital of such a vast, mineral rich country. I had heard nostalgic tales from old "Bechy" hands and, on seeing it for myself, could understand their fond regard for the place.

During my stay much of the talk was of the boom in diamond mining, of vast soda reserves in the Makarikari and Okavango regions and the untapped mineral wealth of the Kalahari which would be accessed with the building of a railway to Walvis Bay. Here was an optimism and *joie de vivre* belying the racial minefield to the immediate South and the poverty to the North.

Having South Africa as a next door neighbour appeared to be both a boon and a bane. National security was virtually assured as a friendly buffer territory was in the interest of Pretoria. Trade between the two was also brisk in contrast to that between South Africa and the more hostile countries to the north. It was not that Botswana felt any less revulsion to apartheid, more a case of pragmatism and knowing on which side its bread was buttered.

The downside was visible every weekend as whites from the South, forbidden to conjugate with black ladies in their own country, and professing to hate all things darker than themselves, crept over into Gaborone to have their wicked way with the local girls.

Air travel in this part of the world always struck me as something of a lottery. Whether flying sideways through a thunderstorm between Bulawayo and Harare, watching an engine throwing out flames while spiralling dizzily upwards into a more rarefied atmosphere over Gaborone, or nervously twitching in the bowels of a clapped out chartered Dakota in Northern Zambia, one thing was always certain; travel was never likely to be dull. It was akin to the passing of an era when Royal Swazi Airlines scooped me up from Lusaka in a sleek new aircraft for my first visit to Manzini and Mbabane.

What a delightful little country the Kingdom of Swaziland turned out to be. Friendly and hospitable, it maintains a proud independence, despite the proximity and economic power of South Africa. Indeed much of its income appeared to be derived from the high rollers who made their way from Johannesburg to the Mbabane casinos each weekend. At times, when out in the Swazi countryside, it reminded me very much of driving through North Wales. The main difference, thankfully, was that most of the locals spoke English in my presence.

The other Southern African country in which I have always felt an inner warmth is Malawi. Driving into Blantyre on a sunny evening, with the sweet aroma rising over a blaze of blue trumpeted jacaranda, is a welcome to set anyone at ease. Whether dining at one of the excellent city restaurants or taking a sundowner high in the Shire Highlands, there was always a curiosity in my mind as to what these well matured establishments would have been like in the days of Nyasaland. Here we were, shoulder to shoulder with modern day Malawis, enjoying their enjoyment, and wondering if it had always been so. Good luck to them.

Further north, in the Malawi capital, Lilongwe, I found the greater preponderance of concrete and plastic to be incongruous in this part of Africa and was always restless to return to the relaxed old world charm of Blantyre and the former capital, Zomba

Two of the great perks for an Africa regional manager are the Indian Ocean territories of Seychelles and Mauritius. Unfortunately for me, the former had chosen its main supplier of telecommunications equipment shortly before my appointment. This setback was more than adequately compensated by the receipt of an invitation to investigate a problem at Rosehill in Mauritius.

I must admit that this was one of two places in the world where I was embarrassed by the fact that I was being paid to be there. The other was the island of Nevis in the Caribbean.

Shacked up and pampered at a spectacular beach resort in Flic en Flac, to the south of the Mauritian capital, Port Louis, I wanted time to stand still. From the moment we touched down at Mahebourg to the moment I left, I was in Paradise. A leisurely stroll around Curepipe, observing the water lilies and giant turtles at Pamplemousse, soaring above mountains and forested valleys the beauty of which defies description, all these were wonderful, and then there were the sun-drenched beaches, the spectacular Technicolor sea life of the Indian Ocean viewed from glass bottomed boats and the breathtaking, ever changing scenery on a drive round the island.

I had always imagined Mauritius to be very British and was surprised to find a stronger French influence right down to the local Creole patois. The size and rivalry of the Indian and Chinese communities were something else on which I had not counted and served as a reminder that, even in the most idyllic places, politics casts an ugly shadow.

None of this affected my enjoyment and there were no politics at Flic en Flac, where half of South Africa seemed to be letting its hair down. No privacy either. One evening while sitting quietly by the floodlit swimming pool, preparing a presentation for the following day, I was vaguely aware of the good humoured activities on the alfresco dance floor beyond the gently swaying palm trees.

After a time the MC coerced one lady and one gentleman onto the floor to start up a progressive statues dance. Boy grabs girl, girl grabs boy, all dance around until the music stops and then freeze. Anyone moving is eliminated. The remainder split and take up new partners.

This was going with great gusto and I felt serenely detached until, "Why don't you come and join in?"

Before me stood a mini-skirted Amazonian blonde with a raucous Transvaal voice which totally denied refusal.

Momentarily setting aside my papers, I allowed myself to be wheeled onto the dance floor and there I rocked sedately to and fro while my formidable partner, by now oblivious to my very existence, gyrated like a whirling dervish. As soon as the music stopped, I summoned all my strength and whipped her off her feet, just as I had done with Tini at Nijmegen. There I froze. Silence descended as the judges scrutinised the assembled statues for the slightest hint of movement.

At this point, in a screech which must have been audible from Rodriguez to Madagascar, my baby burst forth, "Put me down for God's sake, I'm not wearing any knickers!"

As you can imagine, every pair of eyes in Flic en Flac turned in our direction; even the band were craning over to get a better view and what an eyeful they must have got. The MC had no hesitation in announcing our disqualification but, to the delight of all, presented us with a bottle of Stellenbosch for the evenings best entertainment.

At that time I did not know that my warrior princess was engaged to Van der Merwe, an archetypal Afrikaans man mountain. Fortunately for me he was amused too and showed it by inviting me to join them in seeing off the wine.

Following my sojourn in Paradise I made several more visits to West Africa. A particularly dynamic agent in Accra had me chasing up leads which exclusively failed for lack of funds and aid, either British or international. This saddened me once more for, as in so many other African countries, the people deserved better from their own governments.

The Botanical Gardens in Accra were a credit to those who endeavoured to maintain them. Despite almost total penury, they toiled with a pride and memory of their former glory and to a large extent succeeded. I spent several happy hours there.

One venture took me on a drive along the old Gold Coast to Takoradi where I found myself once more in the company of Indian railwaymen, working there as consultants to the Ghanaian railway authorities. Again there was talk of Derby, York, Swindon and Crewe as they recalled their earlier training.

Outside the scene was reminiscent of Kabwe in Zambia. Old steam war-horses were rotting away, bushes sprouting from their rusting bodies. Reports were of tracks disintegrating, lack of funds for maintenance and little or no capital investment. Unfortunately for me, communications enhancement fell well down their list of priorities. And yet the pride was there, the universal pride of the railwayman, making the best of whatever lot he was presented with. The stock that was functional all gleamed under the tender loving care of the engineers to whom it was allocated.

On the return drive, we took a diversion through the northern suburbs of Accra in order to avoid the city centre traffic congestion. As usual there was a widespread brownout and the streets were in total darkness except for the oil lamps and candles burning in the street-side food stalls. At one junction a motorist, sensing danger, tooted his horn. In Nigeria this would not have merited comment but here in Accra the reaction was totally different.

From every direction, from a myriad people who were invisible in the darkness, came a continuous low ululation, "Shhh, quiet please, no noise."

It was so hushed it was eerie and carried overwhelming

power. It seemed to reflect the gentle but determined nature of a humble yet proud community.

At one point I was beginning to feel like a ping-pong ball, no sooner back from one trip than packed off again on another. I even made an unscheduled day trip to Accra, unable to enter neighbouring Lagos on account of a coup which erupted at six o'clock in the morning at the airport as we entered our final approach. After three identical breakfasts and a tedious wait at Accra Airport, we returned on the same Alitalia aircraft to Rome.

This reached a head when, having just returned from Ghana, I was immediately summoned back by our agent in Accra for what he described as a most important meeting. I had been to that neck of the woods too often to expect any miracles and despatched a telex:

"Unable to return to Accra but willing to meet you any time at venue of your choice in Europe."

Back came an immediate response:

"Lew Hoad's Country Club Fuenguerola next Thursday 1000 hours."

It seemed very strange, a Brit meeting a Dane in Spain to discuss business in Ghana, but life is like that, exporting can be fun and at the same time serious.

My experience of Cameroon was of a similarly gentle people, albeit enjoying a much more dynamic economic environment than that of Ghana. There was no axe to grind with Europeans visiting the country. Courtesy and good hospitality were met at every turn. Douala, as with all seaports, was a place to keep one's wits at the ready but vibrant and well appointed nevertheless. I found Yaounde altogether more relaxed. Take away the ubiquitous red dust and the palm trees and one could have been in metropolitan France.

There were reminders lest one forgot that this was Africa. On my first arrival at Douala Airport, I was abruptly refused entry because my visa was not in order. I protested that it had been granted and entered into my passport only the previous day by their embassy in London, but to no avail. The signature was irregular. Not being that easily deterred, I rejoined the queue and this time presented my passport to the same Immigration officer only this time with a Five Pound note inside.

"Is this all you have?" he enquired.

"Yes, apart from travellers cheques," I replied.

He pocketed the fiver and waved me through.

The next reminder occurred at Douala Airport, this time on departure. I had completed check-in and was quietly passing time seated in the departure hall when an elegant, well dressed young lady came over and asked if I would be so kind as to purchase some duty-free cigarettes for her as she was up to the limit herself. She had big appealing eyes and the most angelic smile, so I felt a real mean bastard in refusing her gentle request. It was lucky for me that I did. When we progressed to the next pre-boarding stage she was only the Customs officer inspecting duty-free purchases. She passed me through with a wicked smile but no comment.

Prior to my first visit to Cameroon, I, together with three of my marketing colleagues, had been put through a one month concentrated course to upgrade our French. This was very timely as the first minister I encountered in Yaounde spoke not a word of English.

Having survived this baptism, I flew off to Abidjan in the Ivory Coast where I assumed the same prerequisite would apply. Having spent six hours, including lunch, in the sole company of the Minister of Communications and not having uttered a single word of English, I was staggered when he remarked in the most beautiful Oxford English, "Do you know, Sir, you are the first Englishman ever to have entered my office and offered to converse with me in my own language. I complement you on that."

If only I had known -

North Africa made similar demands on my new found linguistic expertise. I had been very wary of visiting Algeria, both because of its turbulent political situation and because of the seemingly impenetrable dominance of French suppliers there. The reality was markedly different. There was a detectable determination to extricate the country from French dependency and a willingness bordering on enthusiasm to talk to non-French companies.

The cost of eating in the restaurant of the El Djazair hotel was prohibitive and, acting on a tip from a contact at the British Council, I ventured into a suburban *estaminet* not too far from the hotel. Summoning all my courage, I waded into a bowl of fish head soup, generously supported by half a loaf of excellent home baked bread. *De bon gout*, as they say in Cleethorpes.

This experience gave me great courage and I confidently strode round the amphitheatre that is Algiers, sampling the wares of the most unlikely establishments, meeting some interesting and friendly natives into the bargain. Given the right conditions it could once again in the future become a wonderful tourist destination.

My next port of call, Morocco, already was. It was with incredible difficulty that I persuaded the staff at Algiers Airport to allow me to board a Saudi Airlines flight to Casablanca. This was presumably down to the antagonism between the two countries over Western Sahara. Everyone I approached denied the existence of such a flight, which, although published in the timetables, was not flagged up on the airport flight displays. Eventually I fluttered my eyelashes at a sympathetic young lady on the first-class desk who escorted me through Immigration and Customs, summoned a car and despatched me, with my luggage, to a barely visible Saudi 747, parked in the shimmering heat on the far side of the airfield.

Morocco is a delightfully relaxing country. Steeped in history, one has the feeling that everyone who was anyone has been there before you. Most of my business was conducted in Rabat, so Casablanca was more a place to wind down and enjoy. There was never that feeling, experienced in nearly all francophone countries, that the *Caisse Centrale* is watching your every move from the foliage above. If Algeria was trying to free itself from dependency on Paris, in Morocco the determination was even more so.

Finding myself alone late one evening in the lounge of the Casablanca Hotel, the urge to have a tinkle on Sam's piano was overpowering. I treated it with the utmost respect and was carefully closing the lid on the conclusion of my recital when the darned thing slipped and trapped my thumb. By the time I had returned to Blighty it was a luscious shade of purple.

No one believed me when, on enquiring how I had done it, they received the reply, "I trapped it in Sam's piano."

Eat your heart out, Hemingway!

Chapter 6
Injun Country

One of the milestones of my extremely modest career in telecommunications was being part of the team which undertook the connection, albeit temporary, of the first digital telephone to work in the United States. This unheralded event took place in the St. Francis Hotel in San Francisco during a visit with two of my engineering colleagues in April 1980.

We had taken the equipment on a marketing exercise to test the interest in derivative products in the USA and Canada. In simple terms, it combined digital and analogue telephony plus digital data channels simultaneously over a single pair of copper wires: burst mode transmission, or ping pong, to the initiated.

Such was the surprise of our American hosts that they all but choked on their bourbon as one exclaimed, "Man, do you know what you guys have just done?"

Digital technology has come a long way since that day, but it was a very satisfying "first".

My first hard lesson in the cauldron of US marketing was that you cannot sell technology *per se*, no matter how wonderful it may be. The technocrats may love it but they do not sign the procurement cheques. Translate that same technology into an application that wins presidential votes and you might succeed. Thus our mind blowing digital transmission was repackaged on an energy conservation ticket. Now the drums were rolling.

Whilst attending a telecommunications exhibition on my

second day in San Francisco, I had that weird feeling of being totally alone, unknown and not knowing anyone, in a huge arena buzzing with the frenzied activity of thousands of people, each of whom appeared to know precisely what task he or she was expected to perform. I had never been to America and knew no one there personally.

At that moment my name rang out behind me and I turned to confront a former colleague who, I now remembered, had emigrated to California several years previously. Our mutual surprise was immense. After making a quick tour of the various stands while Mike attended to his exhibition duties, I accepted an invitation to visit his company's out of town premises.

"Adjust your chair," Mike suggested, "while I check under the hood. Anything to go in the trunk?"

"No," I replied, "but you'd better check your fenders."

"How come?" he asked bemused.

"Because I'm wondering whatever happened to seats, bonnets, boots and bumpers."

Mike chuckled, "Aaaw, yer gotta use the right terminology here or you'll never get past first base."

The drive over the Golden Gate bridge in clear crisp weather was a bonus I had not expected when I got up that morning. The open plan offices at Mike's company's headquarters were decidedly less thrilling, but it is interesting to reflect that, following the American pattern, our own offices in England were to look just as unappealing and lacking in privacy fifteen years later. They had a computer terminal on every desk in 1980; it would be a decade before that happened in UK.

On the way back, Mike casually dropped out, "I'm not going to take you all the way back to the Jack Tar Hotel. I'll drop you off at the ferry and you can make your own way from there."

"Miserable devil," was the most charitable thought that went through my head on the way to the San Rafael ferry terminal.

As the ferry pulled out into the bay, leaving the grim San Quentin penitentiary behind to port, I began to realise how wrong I was and what a huge favour Mike had done for me. Soon we were passing the Golden Gate with the sun setting low in a cloudless sky. Even Alcatraz did not appear as forbidding as it had always been portrayed.

My attention was diverted by the presence on board of a bevy of attractive looking and exceptionally well dressed young ladies. One could hardly miss them since they were the only other passengers on board. Satisfying myself that they must be some fashionable ladies group returning from a day out, I resumed my appreciation of the scenery across the bay. But the thought recurred that these fillies were way overdressed for a trip on an afternoon ferry. Eventually my curiosity got the better of me.

As a steward came close I asked him, "Who are they?"

"Leave 'em alone, Buddy. They're all hookers on their way to work on Broadway."

I often wondered what they looked like on the return trip.

I have enjoyed some mouth watering delicacies on the waterfronts of the world, roll mop herrings in Volendaam spring readily to mind, and so it was no great imposition to be confronted that evening with an excellent clam chowder followed by lobster Thermidor on San Francisco's Fisherman's Wharf. The place gets way overcrowded in the height of Summer but if you are lucky enough to be there in the shoulder season it is quite delightful.

I used to find eating in the United States a disappointment. Oh yes, they do a fine New York Strip, but it is the same at every restaurant in every town. I've had the very same meal served up in Orlando, Chicago, Indianapolis, Dallas, Seattle, Los Angeles and San Francisco, and always served with the same salad, baked potato and umpteen gut busting relishes. Nowadays, things have changed and you no longer have to find one dish you can stomach and stick to it. There is an infinite choice and it is ever increasing with the influx of Mexicans, Vietnamese, Koreans, Indians, Indonesians etcetera. In fact every goldarn nation under the Sun is somewhere to be found, especially in California.

Candlestick Park fascinated me. That is the cauldron on the south side of San Francisco where tens of thousands converge to watch the American equivalent of rounders and also a version of football where the foot is very rarely applied to the ball. The sporting agenda of baseball, grid-iron football and basketball is a very accurate reflection of the introspective attitude of your average American. Believe me, these sports are massive and adored in the States; the fact that the rest of the world has a totally different sporting appetite does not bother them one jot. The World Series is a pseudonym for National Championships because most believe that the USA *is* the world. Unfortunately, the same can be said of most people's attitude to the rest of the world's activities in general.

I put this theory to the test recently after the US had deposited some seventy Tomahawk and Cruise missiles on Khartoum and Kabul as reprisal for the bombing of the US Embassies in Kenya and Tanzania. Raising the issue the following day with a group of Oakland mothers, I was not surprised to find that half of them were totally unaware of the attacks, most of those who were did not know why and none of them gave a hoot.

"It didn't happen in the Bay Area, why should I care?" cooed one.

I did not embarrass them by asking if they knew where Khartoum and Kabul were, the fact that they were out of State answered that one.

This ignorance of foreign parts was reinforced when a Seattle cab driver asked whether I was a Limey. On confirmation he told me, in a state of high animation, that his mother-in-law hailed from Cambridge in England.

"Jeez, mister, you may have come across her, Mary Davidson!"

If you're out there, Mrs. Davidson, "Hi! How could we possibly have missed each other in this tiny cabbage patch called England?"

To the people I spoke to in Washington State, even New York and Washington DC might as well have been on the Moon. There was a stunning parochialism I had not encountered since my time in Western Australia.

The drive along the Pacific Highway from Seattle to

Vancouver is a cracker. With Peugeot Sound and the Olympic Mountains on the one side and the Cascade Range on the other, there is no pressure to set a new land speed record. It is easy to forget that this is one of the Earth's most volatile subduction zones and could suffer devastating earthquakes and tsunamis at any time, as it has in the past. This stoicism in fact persists along the whole Pacific coast of North America. The people there know that they're sitting astride a time bomb but it doesn't seem to worry them. OK, they're briefed on what to do in the event of a calamity, but I still find their indifference remarkable.

On the first occasion that I undertook this drive, having surrendered the Seattle - Vancouver sector of my air ticket in favour of a luxurious Lincoln sedan, I was so enamoured of the spectacular forest and mountain scenery that I took the car onto the ferry from Horseshoe Bay across to Nanaimo and continued the drive down Vancouver Island to Victoria, the provincial capital of British Columbia. After the warmth of the mainland, the ice cold wind whipping in across the Juan de Fuca Strait came as a rude shock, but it was well worth it.

Of all the cities that I have had the good fortune to visit, there is only one outside the United Kingdom where I would seriously consider permanent residency. That is Vancouver. In time I expect it to become the new Hong Kong as the burgeoning Chinese community continues to invest and prosper, but for the present it accords well with my ideas of what a modern city should be like - clean, cosmopolitan, vibrant, spacious low level housing developments to suit all tastes and pockets, a public transport system that works, good shops and hotels, entertainment and a plethora of good restaurants. In addition it has wonderful parks, easy access to some of the world's finest mountain resorts and above all a feeling that the city fathers are in tune with the aspirations of the citizens. Unfortunately, for many it is the end of the rainbow, as a result of which the city attracts more than its fair share of drifters and hangers on.

My next port of call on that first visit was Edmonton. On the way over the Rockies the aircraft called in at Cranbrook, the scene, shortly before, of a major air disaster. Looking down from the level of the sun kissed mountain crests to the darkness of the Koolemay valleys far below, one could well appreciate the potential for such an event.

After the peace of the early evening flight from Vancouver, what followed between Cranbrook and Calgary was pure bedlam. We were joined by the newly crowned champions of a regional curling tournament together with a host of their supporters. Why they put aisles on aircraft is a mystery when you can walk along the tops of the seats. The whooping and hollering and charging around continued unabated as we climbed between the Rockies, despite the captain's pleas not to disturb the equilibrium of the aircraft.

Drinks were being passed round and consumed at a pace rarely matched outside of Hogmanay. The guy next to me opened his briefcase to reveal a purpose designed interior with pleasure rather than business in mind. In it he had a fine selection of malt whiskies and crystal glasses, each with its own silk lined compartment. Since a refusal would clearly have offended, I downed a dram of Laphroaig while enhancing my hitherto dubious stock with a reference to my links with Scotland, the birth-place of his beloved curling and his ancestors.

There are times when I have brought myself to tuck away a thirty-two ounce Angus rump. You need a large appetite and an empty stomach and you have to be in the mood. Never in my life had I seen anyone tackle a seventy-two ounce steak, but I did in Edmonton. Seventy-two ounces of best beef and he paused not once for breath.

Expressing my amazement to our waiter, I was informed, "After a week of riding out there on the prairie and living on beans, you'd take that for starters."

The deal was, if you could finish it and all its trimmings you got it free; if not it cost Forty Dollars. It's wonderful how the locals learn to live off the tourists in such places!

The bane of my life on the prairies was static electricity. Every time I entered a hotel lift it was like shaking hands with a Wimshurst machine. Dry climate, nylon carpet, metal button, zap! It got me every time. Regina, the city in the Saskatchewan dust bowl, was the worst, memorable for pain if little else.

Apart from the wind chill in Victoria, the weather had been hot ever since arriving in San Francisco. Each city was experiencing its first warm spell after a very cold winter. The temperature gradient in Winnipeg must have been near vertical. The mercury was indicating ninety degrees as icebergs still trundled down the Assiniboine River.

It was in a Winnipeg hotel that I first tasted the enmity between the English and French speaking communities. Not that there were any francophones to be seen in the television room where a rowdy gathering was tuned in to an ice-hockey match between Detroit and Montreal. One might expect Canadians to support fellow Canadians playing against Americans. One would be wrong. All French-Canadians were fatherless people who perpetrated unnatural atrocities on their mothers. The roof rose three feet every time Detroit stuck the puck in the net. At the final hooter everyone was everyone's friend and drink cascaded down throats as if they had just won the Stanley Cup. It wasn't that they particularly liked Detroit, they didn't, rather that they positively detested all things to do with Quebec.

It occurred to me that we had now traversed British Columbia, Alberta, Saskatchewan and Manitoba and still had not heard a word of French spoken and yet all the signs were dual language. It would continue like this at least as far as Thunder Bay.

The Canadian passion for (ice) hockey was borne out on a subsequent visit to relatives in Vancouver when the ten year old boy of the family went off to his hockey class at the local rink at three o'clock in the morning, that being the only slot available in a twenty-four hours a day hockey school. My daughter Louise used to show similar commitment as she mucked out her horses on cold, windy winter mornings back in Rugby. I guess my winter nights under canvas on the snow swept summits of the Cairngorms came into the same category. Love conquers all.

Before reverting to my reminiscences of the United States, I would refer you to the writings of one William McGuire Bryson, author and erstwhile resident of Des Moines, Iowa. In "*The Lost Continent*," his hilarious account of his travels around the States, he says most of what I ever wanted to say about the people and the places.

One area where I do disagree with Bill is his account of Yosemite Valley which he found tacky and overrun by tourists. Walking through the valley in late season, when the number of visitors has dropped off, unmolested and free to take in the grandeur which Nature has bequeathed, listening to the surge of the Merced River as it makes its way between the towering faces of Sentinel and El Capitan, the spectacular downpours of Bridalveil and Yosemite Falls, that is the stuff of dreams, I loved it.

Like all my peers, I had been raised on a script which made out the cowboys and the US Cavalry to be the good guys and the Injuns the baddies, White Eagle excepted, of course. For some time I had suspected that this was FBI propaganda; my visit to Yosemite confirmed it. Having lived in Paradise for centuries, disturbed only by grizzly bears and other Indian tribes, can you begin to digest the scale of abomination cast on these poor unsuspecting native Americans when they were unceremoniously booted down to Fresno by the US Government forces. Ethnic cleansing? You gotta believe it.

Unfortunately we cannot turn back the clock. If the

valley were restored to Indian tenure today, we would no doubt see within no time the construction of a casino and attendant trappings of modern America. You've got to give that much to the natives, they're fast learners.

One peculiarity of Americans is their willingness to stand 'in a line'. Time and time again I have seen people standing in long crocodiles, waiting an hour or more for a minor thrill of ten minutes duration. You'd think they would be experts at it by now but I have seen eateries with fifty yard queues at half the serving windows while the other half remain empty although perfectly ready to serve. Its no deal if you're not in line! And when you are a member of a line it is an education to listen to the banter- I won't give it the elevated status of conversation - going on around you. It makes your average soap sound positively Shakespearean.

"Did yer get the popcorn, honey?"

"Naw."

"Why?"

"The kid's filled his diaper, Jeez, ain't that elfant big?"

"Sure is big fer an el   Hey, Buddy get back in line!"

That is one crime above all that the unwary visitor must not commit. The line is sacred.

One good thing about the line is that there will never be sexual equality, not as long as ladies have their own loos. At some of the theme parks, in high season, the lines for the ladies rest rooms are so long and slow moving that they have to rejoin the line almost as soon as they emerge from the previous visit. How they cope with Delhi belly, I don't know.

If the line is sacred, what about the cap?

I was sitting at a communal lunch table in the garden of the Vittorio Sattui winery in California's Napa Valley, dressed smartly but casually in sports shirt and shorts. I was also sporting a bright orange cap given to me by my wife's brother-in-law, a sailor with the US Navy, during a visit to his base in Atsugi, Japan. The logo on the front of the cap stated:

"COMMANDER FLEET AIR - WESTPAC".

I thought it made a pleasant change from the usual *"DODGERS"* or *"DISNEYLAND"* which are ten a penny, even in England, but I never expected it to be taken seriously.

It was.

A very genial and well presented American lady, I would guess in her mid fifties, so not yet qualified for senile dementia, leaned across the table and gushed, "Gee, Commander, what does WESTPAC mean?"

Flattered by the mode of address, I informed her in my best Westpoint accent, "Westurn P'cific, Ma'am."

"Gee, Commander, it is so good to meet you. What are you doing here?"

Not wanting to be rude or spoil her day, I replied, "We all need our vacation, ma'am."

Turning to her husband who was sitting on my left, she buzzed, "Gee, Hubs, doesn't the Commander look real fine?"

I suspect Hubs was more of a hard nosed critter who had

known from the outset that I was a two-bit Limey jerk who was enjoying playing his star stricken lady along.

"Yer gotta be mighty fine to command Fleet Air," he responded with a poker face.

I was beginning to like the guy already.

"D'you know, we only ever met one other Commander," she persisted, " that was in San Diego five years ago. Gee, it's been a real honour and a real pleasure talking to you Commander."

By this time her Hubs had taken her by the arm and was halfway through the vineyard.

Next day, in Monterey, I purchased an authentic Australian bush hat. So far no one has mistaken me for Crocodile Dundee, but I live in hope.

For the Brit on vacation, the United States is good value. Everything is cheaper, more abundant, better presented and simply inviting you to take part. Probably the best value I have encountered is the Hall of Fame at the Indianapolis Motor Speedway circuit. Would you believe it only costs five dollars to enter. For the same grade of venue in the UK you could expect to quadruple that at least. There you can inspect every car that ever won the Indy 500, even sit in some of them, sit through some spectacular film shows and watch and smell the cars in practice, if any happen to be out on the track. I'd never heard of Al Unser but his ghost hangs heavy thereabouts.

That's America, not only bigger and better, but better value too. I still have not come to terms with why, in Britain, I have to pay fifty per cent more in sterling than what I pay in the USA in dollars at the likes of McDonalds and TGI Fridays for an inferior product and inferior service. I restock my wardrobe on the cheap and travel either by public transport or by hire car, all at a fraction of the British cost. Why? Our American peers have far superior employment packages and much more disposable income. Somebody somewhere is being taken for a ride.

One disconcerting feature of America with which I have difficulty in coming to terms is the absolute power which individuals assume when given any authority, no matter how exalted or menial their position may be. I guess this goes back to the days of gun law when the bullet brooked no dissent. It is evident in the attitude of police, immigration officers and such uniformed establishments and right on down the employment scale. If they have been given orders and think that they are in the right, there is no room for discussion, no matter what extenuating circumstances there may be. Humour, UK style, is positively dangerous in these situations.

This manifested itself when two colleagues were returning on foot one night to their hotel in Honolulu after dining at a city restaurant. The wailing of sirens did not give rise for particular concern; it is a regular night-time feature of all American cities. Before they knew what was happening they were ordered at gun-point to reach and spread. Asked for their names, Jack Kennedy responded first and immediately had his legs kicked out from under him.

"Funny guy, huh?"

Having left his passport in his hotel, Jack spent several uncomfortable hours in the slammer on suspicion of armed robbery before it was accepted that his name really was the same as that of the former President. A more docile, co-operative gentleman you could not have wished to meet.

Another case in point was the barman in a top rated Kissimmee hotel, on the evening of my daughter Louise's wedding. Having offered to buy her old Dad a drink, Louise placed her order at the bar.

"Show me your ID," snarled a particularly abrasive bartender.

"I am a guest here. We're celebrating our wedding reception," she truthfully stated, not that any normal person could failed to have noticed her bridal attire.

"I ain't serving you without ID," he continued.

By this time my curiosity had been aroused. Louise produced her UK constabulary identification from her purse.

"That don't mean nuthin," barked Grumpy, "British cops ain't got no authority at all here in the State of Florida."

By this time Louise was most upset and had abandoned any thought of a celebratory drink. After she had retreated to her room I asked the barman what it was with him.

"She don't look like she's eighteen and I ain't gonna get myself in no trouble. I need to see is her ID, her passport."

I was exasperated.

"For your information she is twenty-two. If you wanted to see her passport why did you not ask to see her passport, politely, instead of ruining the poor kid's big day?"

"Hell, man, I'm paid to pour drinks, not be nice to people."

He was fired the same evening.

I guess this is one of those cross cultural problems we find so hard to adjust to. Because they are white and speak a similar tongue, Caucasians on both sides of the pond expect their opposite numbers to act and react in similar fashion to themselves. Life just isn't like that. Just as there are profound variations between European nations, Americans eat and dress differently, have different tastes in entertainment and humour. What is brash, stupid or offensive to one can be normal behaviour for the other, and it cuts both ways.

Unfortunately the British concept of a typical American is drawn from two elements, the American tourist and the entertainment industry. The reality is quite different. Anyone who has visited Stratford-upon-Avon in Summer will have seen Wilbur, the larger than life tourist, decked out in his Stetson and psychedelic shirt, chewing on his cigar and stating the obvious in stentorian tones. Alongside trots his little lady, hair dyed green or orange or blue or whatever hue is flavour of the month. Nowhere from Florida to Washington State have I come across a Wilbur on home territory. They must keep a colony of them in Langley or somewhere for release into the World when the occasion demands.

I must admit I did see a near replica at Dallas-Fort Worth Airport. The tannoy screeched out for a Mr. Ewing, passenger to San Antonio, to report to the American Airlines information desk and up bobbed a dead ringer for Southfork's J.R., complete with cigar (unlit), ten gallon hat and hide boots, set off with decorative spurs. He had all the appearance of an undercover agent or an off-duty tourist, or both.

One phenomenon you only see in the States, one which we are thankfully spared in Europe, is the gaggle of absolutely grotesque, outsize individuals who cannot stop stuffing their faces with popcorn, fried chicken, hotdogs, burgers and whatever else comes to hand. At 280 pounds I'm big and overweight but at the side of some of these Gargantuas I feel a comparative midget. The theme parks are full of them. I might feel some compassion but they keep on gorging until their legs can no longer support them. Not that they seek my compassion. They all look as happy as Larry and oblivious to their predicament.

For sure, it is a continent of contrasts, the biggest *potpourri* of humanity within a single nation on the planet. One thing I do know; I shall never turn down the opportunity to visit the USA or Canada. Whatever idiosyncrasies their people might display, they've got hearts as big as buckets and they can certainly teach we Brits a thing or two in the art of hanging loose.

Chapter 7
Filipino Frolics

"Mabuhay!" had been the welcome when I was bedecked in a lei at the ramshackle terminal that was Manila Airport in 1969, while in transit from Hong Kong to Sydney.

"Mabuhay!" was again the cry when I arrived in the ultra modern Benigno Aquino International Airport in October 1989.

Never can there have been a people who have remained so cheerful in the face of one catastrophe after another. Whether it be natural or political, economic or personal, you can always bank on the Filipino to come up smiling. They must be the most sanguine people on Earth and precisely what I needed at that particular time.

1989 had been a particularly bad year for me, the nadir of my life. It started tragically when George, my younger sister's husband ran out of road in Glen Ogle in the first week of January. That was followed immediately by my mother being taken into intensive care at Glasgow Royal Infirmary with varicosing of the oesophagus. That same week my wife, totally unexpectedly, decided to seek pastures new and I was left in a daze, wondering what calamities the remaining fifty-one weeks held in store for me.

There were two ways to deal with this predicament. One was to take up residence at the bar of my local inn; the other was to build on the wonderful support of my family and friends and get to grips with the situation. Thankfully I chose the latter. From January to September I buried myself in work, burning the midnight oils night after night at the office, taking only one short break to collect my thoughts in the Yorkshire Dales. During this time I returned from a bracing walk up Great Shunner Fell to be told that Mum had mercifully passed away.

The director to whom I reported at that time had come up through the personnel channel and was quietly perceptive of my turmoil. It was manna from Heaven when he called me into his office and asked whether I would be interested in taking on the management of the company's commercial interests in Manila. I had my wits sufficiently about me not to accept until the terms of the offer were right, but burning inside me was the determination to recreate my life and this was the ideal vehicle on which to start.

If ever a fillip was needed it was there on the faces of Tina, Vivian and Nick, my new staff in Manila. They fell over backwards to make me feel at home, organising my apartment, my maid, my furniture, even my pots and pans. They remained like that until the day I left, three years later.

When I had been pondering back in January that year as to what might lie ahead, I had not counted on The Philippines, less still on the attempted coup which took place within a month of my arrival. The core confrontation took place in Makati, the commercial centre of Manila, and my apartment was right there, bang in the centre of Makati. We had rebels in the basement, the regular army in the office block across Legaspi Street and bullets ricocheting in all directions.

The punctured corpse of a taxi driver lying in the street outside underwrote the fate of anyone venturing out of the building. Snipers' bullets awaited anyone raising their head above the parapet of the roof above.

I was on the fourth floor. Up on the ninth, immediately below the roof-top swimming pool, was a wild, bearded textile manufacturer from North Carolina who, deprived of his golf and dice, spent most of the insurrection in horizontal mode above a shapely Sri Lankan magazine executive. By his bed stood a loaded harpoon.

"First gook past that door gets it!" he drawled, like a latter day John Wayne with beery bravado.

No mention was made of the second, third and fourth after his weapon - the harpoon, that is - had been discharged.

The British stiff upper lip is useful up to a point in these situations. While the Military Attaché from the British Embassy was directing security operations for the British community, His Excellency's lady wife relieved the tension considerably by interrupting the airwaves to ask whether there was anyone for golf at Camp Aginaldo.

On being informed that the rebels were occupying the front nine she blissfully enquired, "How about the back nine?"

There did not appear to be any takers.

After five days, during which the only contact with the outside world was to answer the door to respond to the rebel soldiers' pleas for food and clothing - they actually said "Thank-you" and meant it, when it was they who stood with loaded guns! - there came a temporary and tentative cease-fire while terms for a resolution were discussed. Taking advantage of this, but acutely aware of the snipers still located on the adjacent rooftops, a neighbouring Ghanaian and I decided to make a dash for it in his Mercedes. After half a mile we passed through a regular army cordon and found life beyond to be going on as if there were no conflict on this planet let alone half a mile down the road!

I spent the next week at the Sheraton Hotel in the charming company of Paul Potassi and his wife being dumbfounded by some top class prestidigitation.

Travelling to any distant country is something of a culture shock, not least to an unsuspecting Briton arriving in The Philippines. I very soon realised how little I understood of the country and its people. Firstly, I had expected the English language to run a very poor third to Spanish and the native tongues, of which there are several. In fact I was surprised to find that, in Manila, Tagalog was the everyday language of the people, English was the *lingua franca* of government and business and Spanish was rarely heard, except among those of Spanish descent who treasured it as a mark of their gentility and breeding.

Therein lay another surprise. The Philippines is the only country I have come across where *mestizos*, those of mixed race, are held in higher esteem than the full blooded natives. Whether part Spanish or part Chinese, there was definitely a degree of deference.

I met the lady who was to become my new wife whilst working in Manila. In fact she was working for Cathay Pacific Airways at the magnificent Peninsula Hotel and I was her passenger. This gave me a whole new insight into Filipino life, in the family, in the community and in business. Before too long we had decided to produce our own little *mestiza*, a beautiful dusky bundle of joy whom we called Lizzy. At the age of fifty-four, it was like reliving my life. One thing is for sure, it certainly keeps me on my toes and I enjoy every minute of it.

I had long been aware of the British reputation for arrogance and there were several fine examples encountered by Marie in her everyday dealings with the international travelling set. It is bad enough to find Brits demanding special privileges in Commonwealth countries. What inspires them to think that they can ride roughshod over the nationals of other countries, God only knows, but some do.

One facet of Filipino culture on which all visitors should be forewarned is *napahiya*, or loss of face. We in the West have scant reservation when it comes to apportioning blame or criticising others. In The Philippines that can be fatal, as many have found to their cost. Whether in business negotiation, day to day management or dealing with domestic staff, tact is of the essence. This has a massive impact on all aspects of life. Even in the most culpable situations, from government down, no one ever appears to be held responsible for anything that goes wrong. Arguments go on and on but no decisions are made. Consequently bad practices fester and rogues survive.

Another Filipino idiosyncrasy which can have far reaching implications for the unsuspecting foreigner is *utang na loob*, the exchange of favours. Once a favour has been accepted, regardless of whether or not it was sought, the donor supposes a moral right to call in a reciprocal favour at any time in the future. This can cause great embarrassment and resentment if such a request is declined.

As in other south-east Asian countries, big business is dominated by tycoons of Chinese descent, although the adverse reaction to be found to similar dominance in Malaysia and Indonesia does not surface so readily in The Philippines. The Chinese community has its own code of conduct and woe betide anyone who breaches it. The most frequent violation against the Chinese is kidnap for ransom, their wealth being well documented, and seems to be opportunist rather than racial.

I became intrigued by the love - hate relationship which Filipinos maintain with the USA. Whilst loudly proclaiming their independence and fighting tooth and nail to rid the country of the American naval base at Subic Bay and, before Mount Pinatubo lent a helping hand, Clark Air Base at Angeles City, these same people were doing their darndest to obtain an American Green Card, giving them the right to live and work in the United States, the Promised Land.

Almost as many as those who satisfy US Immigration requirements seem to go there as undocumented TNT, *tago ng tago*, which translates as 'hiding all the time'. This appears to be accepted by some in the Philippines as an honourable reprisal for past colonisation. To the majority, it simply works, so they do it.

Wherever you go in the world you will find Filipinos. Half of the world's merchant shipping fleet, domestic staff, contract workers in the construction and hotel businesses in countries throughout the Middle East and East Asia, together they make an enormous contribution through regular remittances to the Philippine economy and to their home based families. Even the dubious and far ranging profession of 'entertainer' plays its part. Indeed many of the genuine entertainers excel on the global stage, witness *"Miss Saigon."* Language is no barrier. I have met Filipinos who have adapted to life in Holland, Germany and Italy, acquiring fluency in the respective tongues with great facility.

The national newspapers were a constant source of intrigue, not only to me but to most foreigners. The same old stories were recycled time after time. Pseudo-intellectual debate raged, not only day in day out, but year in year out on the same subjects, with very little discernible effect and very few resultant changes.

Traffic management was a perennial hot potato, as was the securing of overseas aid and loans. The dismantling of the stranglehold which the Philippine Long Distance Telephone Company applied to the national telephone network was always a top priority and I guess it still is. The restructuring and privatisation of Philippine Airways was debated *ad nauseam*. Unfortunately Nero fiddled while Rome burned and poor old PAL went belly up with debts of over a billion dollars before Government stepped in with a rescue package.

Power generation was a problem throughout the presidency of Corazon Aquino. Jaw, jaw, jaw. While they talked the situation deteriorated to the point where everyone suffered eight hours of scheduled brownouts (sorry, blackouts, if you so prefer) a day plus any amount of unscheduled outages. Generator sales escalated until it was realised that the owner of the leading generator company was also head of the Manila Power Authority.

There were wheels within wheels everywhere you looked. Friends, relatives, the same old names kept popping up until one was left wondering if there would ever be any hope for improvement. Failure in one post was no impediment to appointment in another of equal or even higher standing. In fact anyone who exhibited the will and capacity to correct the worst scourges and scams was promptly batted down by those with vested interests.

In such a carefully manipulated environment scams of unbelievable proportions were perpetrated with little or no regulation. One of the finest examples occurred on the introduction of a new national lottery. This employed the latest high security technology and was declared to be totally fraud proof. The first draw was performed in the full glare of publicity by a top ranking military officer. The balls jockeyed down, he inspected his personal lottery ticket and promptly announced himself as the winner! There was a mild protest among the populace but the general reaction indicated that it was more or less expected.

It is interesting to observe how the men of The Philippines purport to demonstrate their *machismo*, one might say as a defensive mechanism, for they live in what is fundamentally a matriarchal society. No matter how assertive and aggressive the men like to think of themselves as being, they can only get away with it with other men.

Even being president of a major corporation does not shield a man from his mother's influence and control. The threat to one's inheritance is a powerful persuasion! Many seemingly irrational decisions were better understood when attributed to the invisible mother rather than the high profile executive offspring. This matriarchal influence appears to be exercised quietly but effectively through all levels of Philippine society.

Debt moratoria and restructuring, foreign investment, aid and loans are constantly high on the political agenda. It is small wonder that the Asian Development Bank chose to site its headquarters in Manila.

The main problem with overseas loans during the early Nineties was not so much obtaining them as defining and implementing the projects for which they were earmarked. The Japanese pledged billions upon billions of yen for projects in all major sectors. The Filipinos argued and argued about the implementation until, invariably, the take-up period would expire and the loan offer would be withdrawn. Then there would be acrimony and national self pity and the process would start all over again.

Most of this passed over the man in the street who shrugged his shoulders and let them get on with it. The regular stalwarts of the Prince of Wales pub-restaurant in Makati recognised all the problems, knew all the answers and should have been allowed to run the country with Henry, the owner, as President.

It was in the Prince of Wales that I spent most of my recreational hours. The food was wholesome, the company was excellent and it was only a short walk from my condominium. So congenial was it that my fiancee and I decided that it would be the ideal place to pledge our respective troths. So surprised and elated was Henry that he decided to invest in some redecoration and refitting. What had been a dowdy if spacious committee room was transformed on our behalf into the elegant Hyde Park Room. I guess there is many an Englishman who would like to have been married in his local pub, not many who have done it!

We had a whirlwind courtship with hardly a pause for breath. There is always plenty to do in Manila, a fabulous array of international and local restaurants, genuine five star hotels, each with its own cabaret, restaurants and shops, private parties, sightseeing and theatre. This was the last place I expected to be watching the Western Australian Ballet but perform they did, in spite of the heat and humidity, and they were greatly appreciated. Repertory theatre was well patronised and deservedly so; standards were very high indeed.

Weekends at Tali on the Batangas coast, overlooking the South China Sea, were idyllic. After an eighty mile drive to the busy little fishing port of Nasugbo we would cover the last six miles either on a rough track over the coastal mountains or by boat. 'We' comprised myself and fifteen lovelies from Cathay Pacific Airways, one of whom had a family villa by the sea.

It wasn't long before I had established a reputation for being accident prone. Base over apex on the algae in the pool-side shower, sliding on my back down the balcony staircase, bumping my head on the low joists, all provided painful memories for me and laughs galore for the girls.

One unfortunate encounter between my left big toe and a submarine boulder resulted in a visit to an expatriate physician in Manila. He was a German of dubious pedigree. Some spoke highly of his proficiency, others facetiously claimed that he had honed his skills at the Mengele School of Alternative Medicine. He took one look at my foot and instantly diagnosed a stone-fish bite. Never in a million years and he wouldn't get a chance to practice his amputation prowess. I was off.

On a later visit , when I had been bitten by a hostile hound, he advised me to keep a watch on the offending beast. If it was rabid, it would keel over first, considering the distance from the back of my thigh to my brain. I was a nervous wreck for three weeks thereafter.

He was also the company doctor of one of my friends . On comparing notes his female staff discovered that at their general medicals, conducted individually at various times of the year, the pretty girls were required to strip, the not so pretty were examined fully clothed. I was never sure which group was most offended.

Life in Manila is nothing if not hectic. Whether you are shopping in the city or sitting in one of the perennial traffic jams on EDSA or the South Super Highway, there is always some excitement to catch your attention. Although the rich are very rich, there is a vast base of poverty and hand to mouth survival. This produces incredible ingenuity in ways of making a living. Because of the hot and steamy climate, much time is spent in the open air. Anything that can be traded is traded, on carts, roadside kiosks, by hand in traffic queues, sitting on street corners.

No opportunity to earn a *peso* for the next meal is spurned. From the urchins scratching out reusables on Smoky Mountain, the vast city garbage tip in the Tondo district, to professionals sidelining in food, jewellery or whatever in their city offices, never a trick was missed. I even found one of my own staff doubling as an agony aunt during quiet moments in the office. Local calls, thank Heaven, were free.

The ingenuity extended to the sciences of mechanics and electronics. There was not an electronic circuit board in global existence which could not be replicated in Manila. Patents? Intellectual property rights? They look at you and laugh.

Most of the taxis were Japanese discards, ranging from the clapped out to downright derelict but, whatever the condition, downtime was negligible.

Vehicles bounce down the streets on bald tyres, smoke belching from long defunct exhausts and with engines and bodywork held together with a wing and a prayer. Occasionally Government has a purge and tries to do something about it, but in the words of Chairman Mao, when the wind blows the grass lies low. As soon as the heat is off, they're all back again, horns blaring, arms waving, insults flying in a deafening crescendo which proclaims, "Out of my way, I've got a living to make."

The multi-hued jeepney, festooned with slogans and memorabilia, loaded to the gunwales with jostling, animated passengers and careering through the traffic like a dodgem at a fairground, is a perfect reflection of the pace and style of life in the *barrios*. Those who could not squeeze inside travelled *sabit*, hanging on the back step in death defying posture. I nearly choked when I saw one of our own Scottish engineers being swept through Mandaluyong in such an attitude.

One of the first things on which a Filipino remarks on arrival in an English village is the absence of people. At home, as in all tropical countries, the house is for sleeping in, the street is for living on. In many of the poorer dwellings they sleep in shifts round the clock.

Ingenuity cannot keep pace with this lot. Concrete is poured into new roads but this only transfers the bottlenecks. Concrete is poured into high rise buildings but this only attracts even more into the rapidly swelling metropolitan population from the rural towns and villages, let alone the rocketing number of vehicles which overwhelm the already saturated roads and car-parks.

The people cope with this remarkably, never flinching against the increasing difficulties. However, put a *peso* on the price of a bag of rice or a gallon of diesel and the whole nation will revolt. They know their limits and it is admirable how they manage to survive within them.

I had a wary dislike of elevators. There is something about elevators in less developed countries that has an immediate impact on Europeans. We tend to be non-tactile and like our personal space. In The Philippines, as I had found in Africa and India, no quarter is given. Bodies crowd against you without a second thought and the jostling and proximity can be quite disconcerting to the uninitiated.

The other striking difference is that the elevator in business premises is always occupied, stops at every floor and is always proceeding in the opposite direction to that in which you want to go. All day and every day an endless procession of messengers, vendors, cleaners and people seemingly incongruous to the function of the building sallies up and down, often only travelling between adjacent levels.

Queuing is not recognised. You see the doors close and take comfort at being first in line for the next elevator only to be jockeyed out of the way when it eventually arrives. Degrading as it may be, there is only one option; when in Rome do as the Romans do. I hoisted one particularly rude intruder by his sweaty armpits and deposited him outside the cage one day. Without any reaction whatsoever he was back inside before I was. I felt like King Canute. I suppose it is their survival instinct.

Leaving an air-conditioned apartment to be chauffeured in an air-conditioned limousine to the air-conditioned restaurants or shops, an expat is insulated to a large degree from life in the raw, but there are still plenty of annoyances to remind you of where you are. Having at last found the driver, probably snatching a snack, or *merienda*, with his peers in some remote corner of the steaming basement car park, having spent an hour in traffic while travelling half a mile and having at last made one's purchases, there follows the pantomime of paying and leaving the shop.

In the city department stores, each till is staffed by at least five assistants, one to check the price, one to ring it up, one to check that the price rung up tallies, one to do the packing and one to release the goods. It is rare to find that this group operates as a team. This is excellent for queue building. Protests only prolong the agony. After a succession of mix-ups and delays you finally take receipt of your purchases.

But you are not out of the shop yet. Oh, no. There is still the security guard to be negotiated, the universal checking of bags and receipts. If you were carrying a bag on entry, you will have been required to deposit it in a security area by the door. This means that you do not have the option to leave the store by a more convenient exit for your next port of call. I tell you, it's easier to send the maid or the driver shopping and turn a blind eye to the total price and lack of change.

Leaving a restaurant can be equally frustrating. You call for your bill, wait an eternity for it to arrive, tender your money, wait another eternity for your receipt and change to return, and leave having forgotten what you had to eat, let alone whether you enjoyed it.

The only places where expatriates did not seem to get frustrated were the bars. Well lubricated on the exceedingly good San Miguel beer - much better than its kin in Spain - and debrained by the constant assault of the disco music, erstwhile well disciplined aliens melted like butter under the charms of nubile, bronzed maidens as they gyrated, scantily clad, right in front of their noses.

The Philippines is world renowned for its abundance of beautiful girls; here at the bars they are readily available. Immediately bestowing their charms on any new arrival, their demands in the way of drinks are modest in the extreme. For those wishing to retire early, an equally modest 'bar-fine' would secure the release of the chosen maiden and a further trifling sum would secure her companionship for the night. Word has it that the girls enjoy it as much as their paying customers.

British wives, aghast at their own inability to control the philandering of their men folk, referred to the bar girls as LBFM's - little brown f---ing machines. If ever there was a case of supply outstripping demand this was it.

The prize offering for the gullible was, "Virgin from the Province, Sir, very cheap."

The same 'virgins' appeared time and time again!

As with all countries, the capital city is not an accurate reflection of life in the country at large. Travelling to the provinces reveals a country and people of much greater serenity than is to be found in Metro Manila. But you still have to be careful.

During my period of residence the countryside was infested by the communist National People's Army. Anything Government or in support of Government was a legitimate target for the NPA. America and Americans were Enemy Number One. Just as to a European everyone from East of Suez looks alike, to a Filipino anything Caucasian is American.

For this very reason it used to scare the pants off me when young kids waved to me in passing, shouting, "Hi, Joe!" For God's sake, do I look like an American?

We were also involved in improving the national infrastructure. Although this was on behalf of a private company, the telephone network was seen by historical precedent as a Government undertaking, regardless of the progressive deregulation up and down the country. To this extent we had to take security precautions when working or travelling in the provinces.

On one trip with family and friends to Laguna Province, we passed through Pagsanjan, home of the magnificent rapids which provided the film setting for *"Apocalypse Now"*, only to find the road closed due to the collapse of a bridge. The alternative route took us up over the mountains where we revelled in the scenery. So beautiful was it that we decided to picnic there on the way back. It was sobering to read a bulletin, issued by the American Embassy the following day, that that particular road was strictly off limits to American personnel because of intense NPA activity in the area.

The NPA were not the only cause for concern. Tectonics play a far more serious role. It is here that the mighty Pacific Plate is forced down under the rising Philippine Plate, giving rise to a wide range of natural hazards, including typhoons, earthquakes and volcanic eruptions. The Pacific Ring of Fire is the geological reason for the very existence of the Philippine Islands.

Typhoons one expects every year, even super typhoons, and pretty nerve-wracking they are too. The wind, rain and accompanying floods are bad enough but the wind blown corrugated iron sheets and other flotsam, spinning through the air from the roof tops of high rise buildings like demented Frisbees, are ample reason to stay indoors. Earthquakes are even more worrying.

My first Philippine earthquake registered a mere 6.8 on

the Richter scale. I was engaged in telephone conversation with a business associate when it started.

"Are you experiencing anything strange?" enquired Colin with the laconicism that only a man from the Caicos Islands could aspire to.

"I certainly am!" I responded as my desk bounced across the office floor.

Not wishing to prolong the conversation, I shot out of the door behind Tina, Vivian and Nick and skied without stopping down four flights of stairs. It struck me as strange afterwards that we had passed several Japanese going in the opposite direction, heading for the roof.

Standing on shuddering concrete out in the open was like standing on the surface of a bowl of boiling porridge. The continuous crashing of glass from shattered windows was unnerving, but there was no panic. The Filipinos around me chattered and took up position away from the tall buildings but acted throughout with an amazing calmness.

Was this the big one? They all agreed it was but there would undoubtedly be aftershocks of lower intensity.

"Nice to know that Nature is so predictable," I thought.

But that's the way it was and order was soon restored. Not so in Baguio, to the North, where the Hyatt Hotel had collapsed like a deck of cards with several fatalities, but there in Manila they took it all in their stride. Normal life resumed the following day.

An altogether more spectacular event was the eruption of Mount Pinatubo, a volcano which, for all practical purposes, had been regarded as extinct. There was plenty of warning by way of steam emissions and seismic activity that something was afoot; the conundrum was when and what magnitude.

Badoom!

When she went the whole world knew about it. Pumice dust six inches deep fell on my balcony, seventy miles away. To make matters worse the intense eruptions were accompanied by Typhoon Yunga. To the poor wretches who lived in its shadow or in the path of its flows of boiling lahar, it was Hell on Earth. Blackness, falling rocks, rain drenched ash, howling winds, boiling mud, it must have seemed an eternity before any semblance of order was restored. If the Americans had harboured any doubts about the abandonment of Clark Air Base before, their minds had been made up for them now.

The slopes of Mount Pinatubo had been inhabited by one of the few remaining aboriginal peoples of South East Asia, the Aetas. It struck me as amazing that in a country of seventy million people there could be a tribe who lived completely isolated from the rest of the population. It reminded me of Bishop Auckland. To the Aetas, Mount Pinatubo was home to their god. They had long resented mineral prospectors drilling into their holy mountain and had been predicting a calamity when their god took revenge. Vulcanologists are still not certain whether their might be some truth in what the Aetas were predicting, a bore hole providing an initial entry path for water or an escape route for magma and gases.

When Taal, a volcano with a much more recent history of violence and death, started to produce seismic tremors a short while afterwards, there was considerable trepidation.

Fortunately Taal's activity subsided but it came as a timely reminder that the Ring of Fire can erupt anywhere and at any time.

I came across some of the displaced Aetas on a trip to Subic Bay in 1997. They reminded me of edge-of-town Aborigines in Australia, in strange surroundings, confused, neither civilised nor isolated. Two streams flowed down through their forest camp. One they used for washing in, the other provided drinking water. That, I thought, was neat.

One group was honing its hunting skills, taking pot shots at a tin can with bows and arrows. Pretty formidable marksmen they were too. To a background of titters and chuckles, a bow was thrust my way. This I could not resist, hailing as I do from Nottingham. They were amused as this white pig from goodness knows where lined up his arrow and prepared to make a fool of himself. Magically the can wheeled away with my first and only shot. The Aetas were highly excited by this and exhorted me to repeat the feat.

Knowing from tricky mornings in my Managing Director's office how to get out when I'm winning, I handed back the weapon saying, "Robin Hood," by way of explanation.

Clearly fame travels far for they all bounced up and down with huge grins chanting, "Robin Hood, Robin Hood."

All I needed was a costume in Lincoln green and I could have been adopted as an Aeta!

One of the areas which suffered heavily on account of the Pinatubo lahars was Angeles City. Prior to the eruption it was the main feeder centre to the massive Clark Air Base.

Running adjacent to the southern perimeter fence of the base was The Strip. Very aptly named I would think, judging by the range of entertainment on offer there.

At one point we became excited at the prospect of overlaying the telecommunications in that part of Angeles City. I even investigated the tariffs at one of the better looking hotels in the district in preparation for the arrival of our field staff, some of whom would be fresh out of UK and in for a real culture shock.

The proprietor turned out to be a worn out looking native of Clacton-on-Sea who greeted me with mild curiosity and little warmth.

"One hour or three hours?" dribbled mechanically off his lips.

When I explained that we were considering his palace for legitimate residential purposes over a lengthy period he was thrown into some turmoil.

"Christ!" he muttered, "Never had a request like that. Have to work out some rates."

My imagination was working overtime on the nocturnal atmosphere of this place. Eventually he came up with some figures which I managed to get discounted by fifty per cent for a stay of three weeks or more. I knew that once our guys were installed therein it would be the devil's own job to get them out in less than three weeks.

In the event our plans were overtaken by events, not so much the effects of Mount Pinatubo as the withdrawal of the American Air Force from Clark Air Base. Angeles City went dead.

A similar pattern of events took place at Olongapo.

Heavily affected by the pumice fall from the volcano, Olongapo was devastated by the departure of the US Navy from Subic Bay. A large proportion of the population was employed directly or indirectly in servicing the naval base; an even bigger proportion of the inhabitants was dependent on their earnings. A mass migration of "entertainers" from both Angeles and Olongapo made its way to Manila and beyond when the Yanks went home.

One of the saddest results of the withdrawal of the US forces was the handing over of Camp John Hay at Baguio. This was a wonderful experience if one was lucky enough to receive an invitation to spend time there. High up in the mountains with a climate so much cooler and drier than Manila, it was a veritable oasis.

Breakfast at the nineteenth was a pleasure in itself, looking out over the carefully manicured golf course with its variety of plants and palms. The Texas steaks were as good as I have tasted anywhere, their quality perhaps enhanced by comparison with what was on offer in the rest of the country. There was even a beautiful Honeymoon Cottage which, I understand, was well patronised, and so it deserved to be.

Baguio itself is a beautiful town, its streets lined with pine trees and with a great deal of tourist enterprise. Even the beggars have panache, clinging to the steep rock faces and catching the hail of tourists' coins in butterfly nets. Rarely do they miss and they are never satisfied!

The airport runway has to be seen to be believed, a horizontal strip clinging high up on a mountainside. Even Kigali, where the runway is sited atop a mountain ridge, is put into the shade by Baguio. It is the aeronautical equivalent of bungee jumping.

Another Philippine city which I would be delighted to revisit is Cebu. Steeped in history and with a friendly relaxed atmosphere, time is needed to explore the many attractions of this capital of the Visayas region. Magellan must have been prescient when he made Cebu his landing point in the Philippines. It is as different from Manila as rice is from potato.

One feature of Cebu reminded me strongly of the North West of Scotland.

We used to say, *"God owns the World and all that it contains, except the Western Isles and they belong to MacBraynes."*

In the case of Cebu, for MacBraynes read Aboitiz. There was very little that they did not have a hand in from electricity generation to inter-island shipping.

The finest mangoes on earth come from Cebu, and no wonder when you see how they are protected from wee beasties and whatever. It is an incredible sight to see, thousands of trees with every mango wrapped in newspaper. The hard work is justified, they are the most succulent of fruits and reach market in the finest possible condition.

Across a narrow channel from Cebu is Mactan Island, the eastern coast of which offers splendid beach resorts and coral reefs, also painful memories for both Marie and myself. In my case nobody had told me to duck as I boarded a small boat beneath a rocky overhang. An incoming surge sent me skyward and almost knocked my brains out causing me to fall dazed into the sea.

I was still in a twilight world as we disembarked on a coral shelf some two hundred yards from an adjacent island. This time it was Marie's turn as we worked our way through a minefield of sea urchins. Tropical islands are supposed to be romantic. This one wasn't as I spent the whole duration removing a thousand spines from the soles of her feet. When we returned to Cebu we looked like refugees from Vietnam, one with an ostrich sized egg on his head, the other hobbling on the sides of her feet.

One of our engineers, visiting the tropics for the first time, caused great amusement when he insisted on stopping at a banana plantation in Batangas Province and spent the next twenty minutes hunting for yellow bananas. He was most disappointed and said that his kids would never forgive him for not taking a photograph of yellow bananas actually growing.

Occasional escape from the hurly-burly of Manila was essential if one's sanity was to be preserved. Opportunity for this arose at three monthly intervals by way of trips to Hong Kong or Singapore. The prime reason for such trips was to avoid overstaying the validity of my visa. Not being employed by a Philippine company, I was classed for immigration purposes as a visitor.

If you want to move rapidly from one end of the spectrum to the other, then fly from Singapore to Manila. It is like travelling from Paradise to Bedlam. Much as I liked Singapore, Sanitised City as it was known, I preferred the somewhat more robust atmosphere of Hong Kong, a pleasure which must have diminished considerably since the hand back to China. Even before the handover, the Tsim Sha Tsui of Pamela Fung days had lost a lot of its sparkle. Maybe it is just me growing older. Still, the memories of bawdy Australian revelry in the smoky confines of the now defunct Ned Kelly's Bar will last a life time.

Hong Kong does not even have the awesome Kai Tak Airport any longer. Anyone who has experienced a circuit and bumps through Kai Tak in a typhoon before retreating to Guangdong for a safer landing knows the thrill of flying Cathay Pacific. No other airline would even attempt it.

On one occasion my new wife asked me to take her to see the shops in Kowloon. She was rather surprised when we boarded a bus in Wanchai and proceeded in an upward direction. She had been expecting to hop onto the Star Ferry. She was even more surprised when I led her out onto Lugard Terrace (Lovers Lane) and, from the heights of Victoria Peak, showed her all the shops in Kowloon lying dreamily across the harbour. You have to start in the manner in which you intend to continue.

Back in Manila I had been honoured by an invitation to become a director of the Philippine - British Association. This was a post that I deeply treasured. It gave me the opportunity to meet some very interesting people from both nations.

One of these was the quaintly named Cardinal Sin, Primate of the Roman Catholic Church in The Philippines, and hence a man of great influence. It would be churlish, indeed treacherous of me to repeat the contents of conversations with this eminent gentleman, but I can say with conviction that he has a wonderful sense of humour and a firm hand in history.

Another was Salvador Laurel, one time vice-president of The Philippines. I was never top of the class at history, nevertheless it came as a great surprise to me to find that Laurel knew more about British history, arts and politics than any Briton I had met. How he rued the fact that the Westminster style of government, which he so much admired, could never be made to work in his country, because it needs the will of the people and of the politicians to make it work. Crony capitalism is still rife, long after the demise of Ferdinand Marcos.

During one Phil-Brit luncheon I found myself in conversation with a senior member of the judiciary. I put it to him that, under the Philippine judicial system, which is modelled very closely on that of the United States, if someone had committed a heinous crime and had friends in high places and the financial resources to conduct lengthy litigation, there was a good chance that he could manipulate the appeal system to postpone the day of judgement until his natural demise. He conceded that I was probably correct, but that they were trying to do something about it. That answered a lot of the questions I had been asking myself.

For a nation so rich in heritage and culture, blessed with an abundance of scions brilliant in the arts, science, medicine and religion, it is tantalising and mystifying to witness the endless confusion that reigns in its overall government.

Given sufficient time, say from now to the end of the next ice age, The Philippines may well get its politico-economic house in order. It will be a long haul given the sweet satisfaction of the current hierarchy with the *status quo*. What *is* certain is that the ordinary citizens of that beautiful country will still be smiling, still supporting each other while the pseudo-intellectuals will still be debating the same old issues which appeared on the inner pages of the *"Philippine Star"* today, yesterday and yesteryear.

I love it and would not change it. We in the West take ourselves far too seriously.

Sa muling pagkikita!

Chapter 8
Other Far Flung Places

I have concentrated so far on those territories where I spent most of my overseas time. There were visits to other countries, many of them, and each with a tale to tell, if only briefly.

Who for instance could forget a trip to the Ukraine, shortly after the break up of the Soviet Union. From the comfort (relative) of the Intourist Hotel in Kiev it was fascinating to observe the behaviour of its citizens as they struggled to come to terms with their new found freedom (also relative). I actually felt very safe there and found those Ukrainians whom I had the good fortune to meet to be very warm hosts. But, oh, the austerity. How long will it be before the lower cadres enjoy the same living standards as their counterparts in Western Europe? To walk into a local market and see the paucity of food on offer, the length of the queues (not quite as bad as Disneyworld but getting on that way), to fill ones nostrils with the stench of rotting sauerkraut and experience the utter bleakness of such places makes one realise what an abyss has developed.

Travelling by taxi from the State Circus to my hotel, I was appalled when my driver, a pleasant young man who had just been delighting in the footballing feats of his beloved Dynamo, and was over the moon at my having seen Mikhailichenko legging it down the wing for Glasgow Rangers, was abruptly pulled over by a hefty and uncompromising looking policeman. No offence had been committed. Digging into his pockets, the cab driver pulled out a few rouble notes and handed them over.

Climbing mournfully back into his seat he mumbled, in English, "Why do I work only to feed his family."

Apparently this was a common occurrence as pay day approached. It reminded me of similar acts which I had witnessed in Nigeria and The Philippines.

For all that, Kiev is a fascinating city, sitting high above the Dnepr River, its cliffs riddled with catacombs and its streets wide and chestnut lined. I had to wonder at the opulence of the churches, beautiful as they are, when compared to the penury of the worshippers, a comparison that can be made in any number of poor countries around the world. The cathedral of Saint Sophia is a gem, the beauty of its frescos and mosaics belying the turbulent history through which it has existed. The monastery of Perchersky, from where I accessed the mysterious catacombs, also possesses a wonderful interior. Here was another religious venue where I felt quite out of place as the Russian Orthodox clerics and worshippers went about their respective missions. I could not help but to constantly question what life had been like for these devotees under Stalin and his ilk.

One of the pleasures of grand old cities, for me at any rate, is to sit alone on a bench in a leafy corner, in the case of Kiev in the shadow of Saint Sophia, and watch the passing life. Old ladies busily scurrying along, shoulders drooped under the weight of their shopping bags, meals to prepare before their menfolk come home; young men stepping it out to meet some deadline, obscure to you and me but life threatening to them; old men taking one step forward and two backwards, contemplating every nook and cranny lest something should have changed since yesterday; delivery men whistling chirpily as yet another round nears its completion; gaggles of tourists enthralled with everything from the great arts to cobbles in the streets. One thing missing from Kiev was the carefree frolicking of children. I guess this will come with the appreciation of freedom. Where do I fit into this tapestry of life, I wondered.

I recall once flying over Paris at twenty thousand feet. Down below lay the Arc de Triomphe and the boulevards radiating from it, the Seine winding its way from one horizon to the other, and I thought, down there are millions of people all unbeknown to me. Each one of them believes that his problems are the most important problems on Earth. The Earth from that height is akin to a colony of ants as viewed by a human. If a giant foot treads in its midst, does it have any effect on totality. Do ants have thoughts and feelings and history? Are we humans any more significant than ants? Anonymous people scurrying around teeming cities can evoke similar contemplation. Kiev had that effect on me.

A train journey in January from Kiev to the southern steel manufacturing town of Krivoy Rog is not something that I would readily recommend. It was so cold outside that the Moon looked tropical. By contrast, it was so hot inside the carriages that one had to strip off, there was just no way of keeping comfortable. I compromised by standing at the junction of two coaches where an icy blast screamed through the corrugated awning and passed a large chunk of the journey stepping backwards and forwards between the furnace and the refrigerator. If you're doing research into colds then give me a call.

On the return leg, the gentlemen from the steel works had provided an abundant hamper containing cheese, ham, bread, fruit, champagne and two bottles of excellent Stolichnaya vodka, a veritable feast in Ukrainian terms or anybody else's for that matter. This is obviously the answer to the vicissitudes of temperature on Ukrainian trains. Before the temperature inside the carriage could reach boiling point, my colleague Dave and I had eaten sumptuously, severely damaged the contents of one vodka bottle and drifted into a contented state of hallucination where I might as well have been swaying in a hammock beneath an azure sky on a Polynesian island. Suddenly a coconut dropped on my head and I jumped up to the jolting of brakes and couplings, realising that the iron monster was decelerating through the outskirts of Kiev.

Quite different, at the other extreme in fact, was Colombia which I visited within weeks of my return from Ukraine. In Bogota I did not feel safe. Kidnappings were taking place with disarming regularity and there was grave doubt as to who was in control of the country. The goalkeeper of the national football team had recently been arrested for paying a ransom to secure the release of his son. Anyone with a market value was vulnerable. A journey from Cali Airport to the city centre was undertaken in a car with darkened windows and there was no hanging about at all in the city.

Much as I would like to have explored the country in safer times I felt relieved on my departure. I did rejoice in crossing the Andes for the first time in my life, with magnificent views of the Cordillera Central, and enjoyed the company of my Colombian hosts but felt anguished that civilisation can become so distorted.

Security was not a problem in Japan. I walked for hours around the streets of Tokyo, partly because I was fascinated with everything I saw, partly because I could make neither head nor tail of the directions in the Underground. Not a sign was to be seen in English or any other language intelligible to me.

During my nocturnal strolls I observed with interest the industry of the street cleaners and road repair gangs. How much better our traffic would flow in British cities if such tasks were carried out between midnight and dawn. At that time it certainly had an effect on Tokyo's traffic flow.

On one occasion I thought how nice it would be to purchase a Noritake dinner service in the Ginza district of Tokyo. Must be good value on its home base, I thought, especially when told that it would be shipped to UK free of charge and all damage would be made good. Thankfully I resisted the temptation. On finding the same dinner service on display in the Co-operative in Coventry I was staggered to see that the price was half of that in Tokyo. On drawing this to the attention of the salesman I learned that I could obtain a further hefty discount if I were to go to the Co-op warehouse in Milton Keynes. You could have knocked me over with a concrete cow.

The same was true for everything on sale in Tokyo.

Japanese cameras were cheaper at Dixons; cars were cheaper, even in Britain, and with a much higher specification than the domestic models.

Food must be cheaper everywhere else in the world. I was embarrassed to eat at the New Otani Hotel, knowing what a skinflint my Financial Director was. The *tepenyaki* smelled delicious and the *sushi* looked irresistible, but resist it I did. Breakfast became the main meal of the day, hash browns, sausage, bacon and scrambled egg, and what a travesty!

The purpose of my first visit to Tokyo was to provide commercial assistance to British Telecom on an exhibition stand. Neither the BT personnel nor I could string two words of Japanese together. We looked on hopelessly as stand after stand was erected, but not a sign of activity on ours. Concerned at the lack of time I enlisted the help of a nearby Japanese lady who had already demonstrated her fine command of the English language.

I asked her for a translation of, "Who is responsible for this?"

Her response went something like, *"Kono tanto no hito wa doko ni i ma su ka?"*

I repeated this until it was indelibly etched in my brain. I then approached a gentlemen perched halfway up a stepladder, his feet clad in two toed boots and his belt festooned with every type of hand tool ever made.

"Kono tanto no hito wa doko ni i ma su ka?" I rasped, stretching to my full height and waving an outstretched arm in the direction of the space where the BT stand should have stood.

What ensued had to be seen to be believed. Down he shot from his ladder, barking orders at every workman in sight. Talk about all hands to the plough, within no time at all the BT stand was erected, wired and equipped. The BT guys could not believe what they saw.

"How in Christ's name did you do that?" they asked incredulously.

"Fluency in the language," crowed I.

That phrase has always remained in my memory. It was to come to my assistance four years later at the World Telecommunications Exhibition in Geneva. While anonymously inspecting the Nippon Electric stand I suddenly became aware of the two Japanese demonstrators discussing me behind my back. I could see that this was the case from their reflections in the glass panel in front of me. I allowed this to continue for a few minutes as I pored over the pamphlets set out, none of which provided any information which was not already in the public domain. I then swung round, radio brochure in my hand, and let it go.

"Kono tanto no hito wa doko ni i ma su ka?" I burst forth, waving the brochure.

Two pairs of oriental trousers were soiled at once. Babbling away in words that to me were totally unintelligible, to which they received a continuous volley of 'Ah-sos' and 'Hai-domos', these two unfortunates supplied me with all the trading figures for the radio division of NEC for the previous year. That was what I was looking for. They must have thought that I had understood every word they had said about me and, judging by their reaction, it could not have been overwhelmingly complimentary!

During the fifteen years between my first and subsequent visits to Japan there had been a suburban explosion which has welded Tokyo and Yokohama into a single megalopolis. I found it suffocating. Soon after dawn the freeways become hopelessly congested. If you leave the freeways you are immediately ensnared in a gridlock. The traffic lights at every intersect only serve to further interrupt the traffic flow. God, who would live in that concrete jungle out of choice? I can well understand why we see so many flocks of Japanese tourists in every other corner of the globe. Even they cannot stand it at home and escape regularly for a breath of fresh air and an arm stretch.

It was with some amusement that, after leaving the city for the tranquillity of the foothills of Mount Fuji, I found the waters of Lake Yamanaka even more densely populated with fish than the city was with people. Still, the signs are there. Small industries are creeping in, housing density is increasing and it seems only a matter of time before the Fuji - Hakone- Izu National Park becomes a suburb of Tokyo-Yokohama and Mount Fuji is merely a smoke stack in its midst.

Throughout my exporting career I studiously avoided becoming a Middle East specialist. There were plenty of colleagues who were attracted to the area. For my own part I did not understand Islam or Arabic, nor did I particularly want to make the effort, and therefore never understood the Arab psyche. Without that you are on a hiding to nothing in trying to do business in the region. My forays into the sand and concrete oases of the Gulf were limited to Bahrain and Kuwait.

Bahrain I remember best for its excellent souk. A centre of seemingly honest endeavour and scrupulously fair trading, I enjoyed the hustle and bustle, never once being put under the uneasy pressure that one can experience in similar bazaars elsewhere. It was fascinating to watch the meticulous weighing of silver, gold and gems, all handled with forceps, weights and balances maintained in immaculate condition. I had witnessed the same precision some years previously on the streets of Lome in Togo in the trading of filigree silverware. I am sure there were guys in the Bahrain souk who could have shaved off my eyebrows while I slept, but they have an unshakeable pride in their reputation for fair dealing.

I was asked on one occasion to apply my commercial savvy to what appeared to be an impasse in the negotiation of a contractual condition forming part of a tender proposal to a customer in Kuwait. This I did and completed the negotiation to the apparent satisfaction of both parties. What I had not reckoned with was that thereafter I was to be deemed a Kuwait 'expert', something I had worked hard to avoid throughout my career. Once you get bogged down in sand, there is no escape and there were still large tracts of this planet which I had yet to explore.

The Kuwaitis were extremely hospitable. They could well afford to be, but that is not to denigrate the time and trouble they always took to make their guests feel relaxed and welcome, even with the Red Guard camped on their northern border. There can be a most irreverent sense of humour lurking behind a *dishdasha*, as I soon found out.

After a night of sampling the finest Scottish malts and *hookahs* burning I know not what, but certainly not Erinmore or St. Bruno, I felt a sense of utter helplessness at three in the morning, squatting by an enormous cloth laden with every delicacy the State can provide, while being pressed to devour the brains and eyeballs of a sheep. A refusal often offends and I had no wish to offend anyone. The looks of anticipation on the faces of my hosts indicated a full understanding of my internal dilemma. I have no idea what I looked like the next morning from the outside. On the inside I felt as if I had spent the whole night upside down on a roller coaster at the Montezuma carnival. I certainly did have an internal dilemma!

I was presented with a *dishdasha*, the free flowing Arab over-garment, on a visit to Kuwait. What purpose it is meant to serve in Wilmslow is difficult to fathom out but it did enable me to set up my wife immediately upon my return. To demonstrate its sartorial appeal, I donned the garment together with a makeshift head-dress comprising a white pillow case and black Alice band. I had acquired a good tan in the Gulf and a pair of Raybans set it off a treat. Passing through the dining room to seek Marie in the lounge, I was amused by the expression on the window cleaner's face as he peered in. His gaze followed me into the lounge and back out into the hall. He was not aware that I was home and was obviously intrigued by the company my wife was keeping in my absence. I'll give him his due, he never passed comment, then or later.

I suppose the most bizarre assignment which came my

way was an invitation to join a Trade Mission to St. Christopher and Nevis. The mission comprised representatives from major sectors of British commerce such as banking, architecture, construction, chemicals and food processing. Our parent company was invited to represent the UK electrical industry. Head Office assumed that this would appeal to their telecommunications company, whose corporate heads lobbed it as if it were a primed grenade at their switching division, whose commercial manager considered it all to be a futile exercise in terms of his products. Anyway, not wanting to offend anyone up the ladder, he summoned me to his office and asked if I would like to break the monotony of commuting to and from Nigeria with a trip to the Caribbean. Now what would you say?

After careful consideration I accepted and then enquired why I was to be so honoured, having no concept whatsoever of telecommunications in the West Indies and being fully aware that none of the Caribbean countries featured on our list of sales targets. He knew very little of what was involved, except to say that it was a complete waste of three weeks of my time, and instructed me to attend a meeting in London later in the week. By the time I took my place at the initial meeting I had already been decreed an expert in power generation and distribution, domestic appliances, street lighting, telecommunications, railways, elevators, air and marine navigation systems, building wiring, and meters for all applications. I denied any knowledge of nuclear engineering and was told that, in the case of St. Kitts and Nevis, I should not worry too much about that.

When it came to pass, we all had a wonderful time. By the time we reached Antigua everyone in the party was on friendly terms with the others. The fact that none of us were in competition with each other and came from fundamentally different fields of business made for relaxed relationships. After circumnavigating several ominous looking cumulonimbi and diving through a gap into Basseterre we were all well into the spirit of the venture.

I was a good listener and made copious notes of the territory's electrical and financing requirements and everyone seemed to be content with my performance. At my own behest I was taken on a drive around the perimeter of St. Kitts. I was able to witness at first hand the parlous state of the telephone links with the outlying villages. Every year, I was told, the cables are destroyed by the heat from the burning-off of the sugar cane. Hurricanes were seen as something of a problem but no one worried too much about the volcano which hovered high above their heads. With Monserrat, Guadeloupe and Martinique just down the island chain, I would have.

It pays not to be too forthcoming on these somewhat abstract occasions with one's companies specific capabilities, as I soon found out. Back at base we had developed what we called the Island Concept. In simple terms we had realised that around the globe there are several thousand islands, many of which have a volcano in the middle and are surrounded by a ring of villages, one of which develops as the capital. By devising a telecommunications strategy for a typical island, you have the blueprint for all similar islands. Both St. Kitts, with Mount Liamuiga at its centre, and Nevis, dominated by Nevis Peak, fitted this concept very well. I had it all worked out in my mind. One evening, at a roof-top cocktail party in Basseterre, I passed on my thoughts to a local telecommunications manager. Before I knew it, he'd introduced the Minister and asked me to repeat my vision.

"Stand there and don't go away," ordered the Minister.

He returned some minutes later with the Prime Minister.

"Please repeat to the PM what you told me."

I repeated my exposition. The PM took my arm and said, "Be outside my office at five minutes before ten o'clock tomorrow morning."

Next morning, at ten prompt, I was shown into the Cabinet Room, where I was requested to repeat to the full cabinet exactly what I had told the PM. My account sent the whole room into animated discussion. Finally, the PM instructed me to return to London, put together a formal Proposal, complete with funding package and submit it to him personally.

I never had the chance to do that because, in the interim, a letter, originating from 10 Downing St., arrived on my desk, having passed through innumerable internal company directors, asking for an explanation. The whole thing rapidly collapsed over the non-availability of Government or commercial funding, allowing the Canadians to move in swiftly and do what I had suggested. Nonetheless it is a good lesson: strike a match and you can start a forest fire.

Chapter 9
On Reflection

Telecommunications is, regardless of the views of the beancounters in Whitehall, an essential element of infrastructure. It is to be expected therefore that, at the outbreak of hostilities, whether in war, a *coup d'etat* or insurrection, one of the first targets, along with broadcast transmitters and airports, is the national telecommunications network. Rehabilitation of these networks becomes a priority at a time when it is considered reasonably safe to do so. That normally requires the assistance of a major manufacturing company from a developed country.

Questions have frequently been asked about the field staff who venture into such theatres at considerable personal risk, or perceived risk. Are they compelled to go? Are career prospects threatened pursuant to a refusal to go?

Having been involved in such decisions, both as a field engineer and in a managerial capacity, I can safely say that I have never witnessed any compulsion. The individual staff member has always had the basic right of refusal laid open to him or her. Propulsion, yes, by which I mean that subtle pressures may be applied. Access to big bucks and high margins are irresistible to large companies and contracts, once signed and legally effective, have to be honoured.

The vast majority of staff who undertake hazardous operations overseas do so of their own free will, either for the money in the form of additional allowances and bonuses, or to establish themselves as good, keen front-line people, willing to go that mile extra on the company's behalf in order to further their promotion prospects. Some even thrive on the adrenaline of excitement alone, charged up and stimulated by the unpredictable rather than succumbing to death by boredom in a humdrum occupation. If you enter a career in export sales or field engineering you must accept at the outset that there will be both rough and smooth assignments.

Sometimes however when the going gets particularly rough, there are insufficient volunteers of the requisite skills or calibre to satisfy the requirement. It is then that indirect pressures can be invoked.

"Others are doing it, why not you?"

Another resort is "You're the only person with the necessary attributes. We are looking very hard in your direction."

I have also heard, "You will be afforded constant protection by the host government and our embassy will be in close contact," where it is the host government itself which poses the biggest threat.

But the most insidious pressure is the silent threat that, if you refuse this assignment there is a high probability that you will not be considered again.

At the end of the day most risks can be controlled. In the most turbulent hot-spots, if you keep your head below the parapet and act according to expert advice and with sense and discretion, you will be unlucky not to survive. But the back-stop is always there; the right to refuse.

In my own case I saw Nigeria as a cross-roads in my

career, I reserved my right not to venture into war-torn Iraq and conducted business in forty-five other territories in the enthusiastic belief that it was all part of the fun of exporting, even trigger-happy Uganda.

It is a common trend among those who tramp the export trail that they start off fresh faced and innocent, full of vigour and high ambition. After a few years of banging their heads on brick walls and listening to the *Been There; Done That* brigade an irreversible degeneration can set in and they finish up either as a bar propper, exiled in some long forgotten corner of the tropics, or as a cynical and disgruntled hack back at base.

There are others who plough a more purposeful furrow, accept the challenges, bring fresh thinking to seemingly intractable problems, enjoy the rewards and go on to establish a fulfilling career on which they can reflect with much satisfaction.

Looking back, I am happy that I can associate myself much more closely with the latter. Never destined to reach the top, I did go some distance, both physically and metaphorically, and am able to reflect with considerable pleasure and with the satisfaction of knowing that I did make some small contribution to improving people's lives across the world.

There are regrets, of course there are. There were situations which, if handled better or if I had listened more closely, would have reaped better rewards both for me and those with whom I have been most closely associated. This is where, in my convoluted interpretation of religion, I believe that Hell is here on Earth. It is the subconscious which haunts you all the days of your life, that plays back those things which you most want to forget and does it at the times when you can least escape its all enveloping power.

But running through all this are two maxims which I fervently recommend to anyone following the same course. The first has long been dismissed by those who see wealth and power as their twin gods.

Man arbeitet um zu leben; man lebt nicht nur zu arbeiten.

You work to live; you do not live only to work. Work can and should be a highly satisfying element of your life, you spend the majority of your conscious hours engaged in it. And to make work enjoyable, at home or abroad, you have to work diligently at it. That sounds repetitive but it is the truth.

The purpose of work satisfaction is tied into the second maxim, on which I was once challenged by my boss on a joint trip to India.

"What comes first, he asked, "your job or your family?"

I actually thought it sad that anyone could be in a position to ask that question.

"My family every time," I responded.

"You're kidding yourself, it's always the job," he went on and he really believed it.

It probably did not do my immediate career prospects a lot of good, but that was of secondary importance.

My family comes before the job.

That had always been a cornerstone of my life, both single and married. I was not going to give the man the satisfaction of justifying the obscene distortion which 'progress' has attempted to foist upon civilisation and which many have assumed with consummate dispassion and ultimate regret.

The two, work and family, feed off and support each other. I know that I could never have enjoyed my overseas endeavours nearly as much without the love, support and reward of a happy family. If I had not enjoyed it, the enthusiasm to persist doggedly after seemingly unattainable objectives in squalid and sometimes dangerous corners of the earth would long since have quenched.

Conversely, the sacrifices made by the family, particularly the long periods of absence in the children's early years, deserve the rewards of love, health, security and peace of mind. Money helps, helps enormously, as does power in obtaining it, but it is always secondary to the family well-being.

I can justify this by reference to examples which I have witnessed personally around the world, some of which I have related earlier. The destitute in India, famine stricken villages in Africa, garbage sifters in The Philippines, the sick, the suffering and displaced refugees across the globe, all are categories with which one would not want to change places. But I can say with some confidence that I have seen more happiness, camaraderie, love and trust in all of these than exists in many of the greed-ridden upper echelons of the developed world. You can strip people of all their worldly possessions but the comforts of family love and trust will survive and help them fight another day.

I recall travelling on the Piccadilly Line from Heathrow

to Green Lane one morning having just flown in from Calcutta. The poverty, disease and squalor there is unimaginable unless you have witnessed it. The Bengalis were buzzing around, each with a task in hand, if only to beg, not a complaint to be heard. Here, I was listening to the abject outpourings of two well heeled, middle aged Londoners, who, between Hounslow and Acton Town, set out every complaint imaginable about the hopelessness of life in Britain, from the pitiful wages in the Civil Service to the rubbish broadcast on the television. There was not a word of joy in what they said; they did not have a good word for anyone or anything.

What a way to go through life, I thought in sorrow and disgust. If they had seen what I had just left they might have had cause for complaint, but the poor unfortunates of Calcutta were not complaining. They were just getting on with life and with each other, grateful when given to rather than moaning when deprived of.

So it has been with me, grateful for a life shared with an endless stream of kind and interesting people. There have been sad moments, regrettable events, but there always would have been, I would not want to change it. I would absorb the downside because I have reached a state of equanimity, peace with myself, with my family and with my friends. I have travelled through life with a smile on my face and still do.

People often ask me which country I have enjoyed most. It is very difficult to say, there are so many contrasts, so many wonderful people and places. It is like the synergy of a tapestry, the whole is greater than the sum of its constituent parts. The most idyllic country would be Mauritius, the most interesting India. The most awe inspiring sight would be flying in the crisp light of early morning past the towering ice walls of Nanga Parbat, *en route* from Amritsar to Tashkent. The friendliest people, collectively, are the Filipinos.

It is an impossible question to answer. It is all in the eyes of the beholder. Another man may have travelled an identical route and drawn quite different conclusions. Above all, wherever I found myself in any of the five continents, the greatest treasure was the return ticket which would one day bring me home to my family.

Of one thing I am certain. In every single country that I have visited, without exception, most of the people whom I have met have been kind, peaceful, loving and welcoming. Man's inhumanity to Man is inconceivable when you meet the ordinary peoples of the World, and yet it continues to happen, tribe against tribe, country against country, religion against religion.

I have come to the conclusion that the overwhelming majority of people in the World are basically good, but far too many are easily exploited and manipulated by a small minority who are either warped or powerfully sinister. This is manifested in the plethora of regional wars and skirmishes which prevail, and also in global scourges such as terrorism, drugs distribution, slavery and prostitution.

Others, particularly in the most developed countries, become the victims of managerial pressure. The competition for increased market share, to maintain margins and reduce costs, produces pressures at the top of every business which are transmitted downwards by fair means or foul creating insecurity, stress and distorted decision making at every level of operation, particularly in higher management. This has the knock on effect of contaminating peoples values and actions towards each other. Just as most criminals do not set out to be criminals, most tyrants at work do not set out to be such. They are pressured into such actions in order to survive. Some zealously cultivate their dastardly art in pursuit of greater glory but very few of them had that intention at the outset. I know, I've seen it happen all too frequently. It wasn't always like this.

I continue to travel, still with an avid thirst to explore fresh fields, while always enjoying revisiting old friends and old places. In this respect I am very lucky in that my wife, now living on the opposite side of the planet from her Philippine roots but still working in the international airline business, is of a similar mind. By the strangest of coincidences, unbeknown to me, Marie had also been resident in Nigeria from 1972 to 1975. Her father was then an expatriate civil engineer with the Nigerian Ministry of Works. Her school was in the next street to ours. From old passports we were able to determine that we visited the American Embassy in Lagos on the same day in 1973. It is remarkable when reflecting over our respective lives how very similar our convergent paths have been and yet having emerged from such markedly contrasting origins.

I believe the word is *destiny.*